Two Grow Up in Dorset

Memories of the 60s and 70s

Jeanette Hardiman

and

Jackie Spiteri

Brimstone Press

Acknowledgements

Our thanks go to Dave Hardiman, Sue Puntis and Maggie Pierce for their honest input and feedback in the early stages of writing the book. Their local knowledge and expertise were invaluable.

Gratitude also to Eric Olsen, Ann Symons, Roger Hillman from Fontmell Magna Village Archive Society, currently celebrating their 25th year, and Gold Hill Museum, for providing countless photos to enhance the publication.

Thanks also go to Keri Jones at This Is Alfred Community radio station who has aired our weekly recordings of 'Two Grow Up In Dorset' for many months. Those recordings have provided the basis and research for this book.

Massive gratitude goes to Mel Thomson from Brimstone Press for his expertise, help and support in getting this book published. Without him, we would have been lost.

The benefit of hindsight enables us to fully appreciate the idyllic surroundings in which we were lucky to grow up. Our memories are full of unforgettable people and places, all of which have been the inspiration for this book.

Lastly, as cousins who spent very little time together growing up, this book has given us the opportunity to realise not only how much we have in common, but also how much we enjoy being in each other's company.

First published by Brimstone Press

www.brimstone-press.com

© Jeanette Hardiman and Jackie Spiteri, 2024

ISBN 978 190638592 7

For our family – enjoy!

About The Authors

Friends and cousins Jeanette Hardiman and Jackie Spiteri grew up in the neighbouring North Dorset villages of Fontmell Magna and Compton Abbas in the 60s and 70s, attending the same schools and many family events. Jeanette's father, Raymond (Ray) and Jackie's mother, Winifred (Winnie) were siblings.

Jackie worked for more than 25 years as a journalist and sub-editor for local publication the *Blackmore Vale Magazine* and now works as a freelance ghost writer.

Jeanette's 38-year career in the finance sector included experience of marketing and communications. She's now involved in a number of voluntary organisations.

This book details the cousins' memories from childhood through to starting work. In 1979, the girls moved away from the area, returning in later years.

Jackie now lives in Marnhull and Jeanette in Shaftesbury.

Contents

Introduction

After writing and presenting a number of well-received podcasts and radio broadcasts for Shaftesbury's local radio station 'This Is Alfred', we decided it would be useful to reproduce our conversations in this book. Our 'ramblings' cover a wide range of subjects including village life, family events, first jobs plus more generic subjects such as pop music, TV and film, food and fashion, shopping, social life and cultural change.

Our book is a snapshot of conversations between two cousins and a reflection of our lives growing up in North Dorset. Much of the content touches on the social changes affecting many people in Great Britain in the 60s and 70s and will appeal not only to those who grew up in rural Dorset, but also to anyone of a similar age.

Our podcasts and radio broadcasts are a relaxed, two-way discussion and we've tried to reflect that chatty and informal format in our book while incorporating some humorous elements.

We hope to evoke memories of a simpler, bygone age for our readers.

Remembering our roots

We all need to remember our past; to find and celebrate our family roots. It is, after all, what shapes our lives today. Whether it's 150 years or merely decades ago, the need to find out where we come from is part of what makes us human.

The lot of the farm labourer in rural Dorset during the 19th century was not a good one and many young men left homes and families to seek their fortune in the land of opportunity across the Atlantic. Most of these young men would never have the chance to return to the land of their birth although, it's never too late for their descendants to reach back through the years and discover where, in a way, they still belong.

The Umbrella Girl

It was a very dull and rainy day in 1979 when there began an amazing reconnection with four boys who had emigrated from Compton Abbas more than a century before.

On her way to work in Shaftesbury, while walking to the bus stop in Compton, Jackie was stopped by a group of Americans who asked if she knew Emily Hardiman. These Oklahoma Hardimans, who were in the UK to discover their roots, had not only found the right village,

but had also found a cousin on their first attempt. Quite some feat in pre-internet days.

After Jackie provided them with directions to her granny's house, Tom Hardiman jumped out of the car and took a photo of her standing in the rain on Chapel Hill, after which she was forever known in certain parts of Oklahoma as 'the umbrella girl'.

That fortuitous encounter led to a close relationship with the girls' American cousins which continues to this day. Their families have enjoyed many happy visits with the descendants of the surviving three Hardiman brothers whose relatives now live in various parts of the USA stretching from Boston to Chicago, Colorado to Texas and Oklahoma to California.

How many of us have regretted not asking parents and grandparents about their childhoods while they were still around? Whether that childhood happened thousands of miles away or closer to home, information about our heritage is so very precious.

In a fast-changing world our descendants will be incredulous, as well as hopefully, entertained, to discover how different life was in the 60s and 70s.

The lane from Capstitch.

1

Village Life

'Shroton Fair weather' was how my mum described the weather on a certain type of autumn day...'

Imagine a childhood where...
The rector is a much loved and respected figure in your life.
Your surroundings are totally safe and secure.
Pleasures are simple but memorable.
The village is your world.

Jackie: The feeling of walking in ancestors' footsteps always strikes me when I visit Compton. Generations of the Hardiman family, stretching back to the 18th century, have made the village their home.

Jeanette: Yes, I know what you mean. Even though we lived in Fontmell Magna, I think my dad's heart always lay in Compton, where he was born.

Jackie: When I round the corner at Incombe on the way from Shaftesbury to Compton and see the 'lanch', that massive grassy hill where we picked cowslips, or when I'm travelling up from Fontmell, spotting the top of St Mary's Church spire among the trees, it always takes me straight back to childhood. The lazy drone of a small plane from Compton airfield reminds me of summer afternoons in the garden. But I suppose it's the village church that holds the most memories, as it's stood unchanged over the decades.

Jeanette: That churchyard's the resting place of several Hardiman relatives including your parents and our mutual grandparents.

Jackie: And so many villagers from my childhood. It's such a peaceful spot. I often sit on the bench dedicated to my mum and dad, and look out towards the downs. Baptisms, weddings, funerals,

St Mary's Church, Compton Abbas, the ancient font, and hassocks embroidered with the names of local fields and flowers by the ladies of the village.

so many times I've walked through that familiar arched doorway of St Mary's. The smell of flowers and polish; the ancient stone font where I was christened; the eagle lectern; the dusty windowsills where vegetables were placed at harvest festival. And I always loved the hassocks in the side chapel, lovingly embroidered by village ladies and depicting old field and flower names such as Whitsun Acre and Monks Mead.

But St Andrew's Church in Fontmell is quite spectacular too isn't it Jeanette?

Jeanette: Yes, it's a beautiful church. And I spent a lot of time there as a child.

St Andrew's Church in Fontmell Magna.

Jackie: The seasons were always marked with annual events in both villages weren't they? The village fete and the Sunday School outing to Weymouth in the summer; harvest festival, then Halloween and Guy Fawkes; carol singing and midnight mass around Christmas; Mothering Sunday, Palm Sunday and Easter.

Jeanette: Yes, and everything was done with wonderful community spirit.

Jackie: A huge part of my memories of Compton include Reverend Chaffey-Moore, our rector. A Sunday School class wasn't complete without him diving into the folds of his cassock and producing some exotic carving or object from deepest darkest Africa or the Far East. And then he'd enthral us with a story about its origins.

Reverend Chaffey-Moore, seen here at a tree planting in Compton's old churchyard, was an important figure in the girls' childhood.

Jeanette: He used to come and talk to us at Fontmell School quite regularly. Everyone enjoyed his stories.

Fontmell's vicar was Reverend Shorton who lived in the vicarage in Mill Street with his family. Of course, back then the vicar was an important part of the community.

Jackie: Reverend Chaffey-Moore taught us to play the handbells which we performed at church services and the village fete. The handbells were kept in a large trunk in the rectory study. The old house was stuffed full of artefacts from his travels as an army chaplain.

Jeanette: And he used many of those items to explain complicated things in a simple way.

Jackie: He certainly did. As Sunday School pupils, we constructed an Easter garden at the back of the church which involved collecting large stones and moss to recreate the Garden of Gethsemane. The crucifix, wrapped in muslin, was placed in the cave-like tomb which

The original Fontmell Magna Village Hall in the 70s.

was sealed with red candle wax. On Easter Sunday the seal was broken to reveal an empty tomb. As a small child, this whole process caught my imagination in a much more effective way than if dear old Reverend Chaffey-Moore had merely read the Easter story from the pulpit.

Jeanette: Gran Hardiman always attended the Methodist chapel in Fontmell. And that chapel was also used as the doctor's surgery a couple of times a week plus, in the 60s, when a chimney fell through the roof of the primary school building, it was transformed into a 'pop-up' school.

Jackie: And the village halls were well used in those days in both villages, weren't they? They were a meeting place for the ladies of the WI; Girl Guides; Beetle and Whist Drives; wedding receptions, not forgetting jumble sales. People queued outside the door to try to bag the best bargains. The ladies from the WI were usually manning the tea urn in the kitchen and the most us children could expect was a weak orange squash.

Jeanette: Wasn't Compton Village Hall also the schoolhouse at one time?

Jackie: Yes it was. My mum actually went to school there and won a scholarship to Shaftesbury High School but, probably for financial reasons, was put into 'service' at the age of 14. In the early 30s she worked at Cross Tree House at Fontmell and Fontmell Parva House. And when she worked at Venn House in Milborne Port, incredibly,

Compton Abbas Village Hall.

on her one afternoon off each week, she'd cycle 15 miles back to Compton to hand over most of her wages to Gran Hardiman.

Jeanette: Unbelievable. Just imagine a 14-year-old being sent to work 'below stairs' these days.

Jackie: And amazing that she cycled all that way on a bike that probably had no gears.

Jeanette: Of course, Fontmell Village Hall was, for many years, the very heart of the village. There was a stage in those days and we'd often watch the local pop group, The Ramblers, rehearse. They were four village boys who we hoped would make 'the big time'. I think they based their act on The Shadows who were such a popular group back then. In fact The Ramblers appeared on a TV talent show once and made it to the final, but finished second to a comedian.

Jackie: You were very lucky to have so much going on in Fontmell.

Jeanette: The villagers were mostly people who'd lived there all their lives. As children, we thought they were all very dull, but looking back now, I can see that those individuals were real characters who must have had such wonderful stories to tell. One of my earliest memories is of seeing Ben Chick, who lived at Blandford's Farm, enjoying bread, cheese and a glass of cloudy 'scrumpy' cider for his breakfast. I think he kept a barrel of that cider under the stairs. The Chicks provided milk for Fontmell and the surrounding villages. In fact, my mum was the dairy maid at one point. The big, silver milk churns were left outside the farmhouse for collection every day.

Jackie: There were some real personalities living in Fontmell. Wasn't there a shepherdess?

Jeanette: Oh yes. She had blue/grey hair, dressed in scruffy clothes and wellington boots and always had a couple of border collies at her side. It was very unusual for a female to be a shepherd back then. She was quite a trailblazer. We also had the Gardiner family, who ran Springhead Estate. Springhead House was like the 'Buckingham Palace' of Fontmell.

Jackie: Grandfather Hardiman and Uncle Jack both worked for Mr Harding on his farm at Compton. He was always known as 'the boss'. My mother worked in the farmhouse, and many villagers, including us, lived in farm cottages. These were the supposedly 'good old days' when landowners employed dozens of farmworkers.

Jeanette: Another legendary landmark in Fontmell is the bus shelter. I spent hours waiting for the number 24 bus that ran between Shaftesbury and Bournemouth. That shelter hasn't changed a great deal, in fact, the same wooden bench is still there. But now there's also a plaque on the outside wall which states, 'This shelter was constructed entirely by local voluntary craftsmen and labour 1956 to 1957'.

Jackie: Yes, these days I think there are specialists who study bus shelters.

Jeanette: Further up the road from the bus shelter, standing at the junction of Church Street and West Street there used to be an elm tree called Cross Tree, also known as Gossips Tree. We often climbed that tree, but at some point it was 'topped' and sadly, in the 70s, it was cut down completely and replaced with the lime tree that's there today.

Gossips Tree, Fontmell.

Jackie: I always envied your lovely pond in Mill Street.

Jeanette: That stretch of water was always called 'The Lake' although it's really just a large pond. It runs down from the Springhead Estate and we spent lots of time there, feeding the ducks and swans.

Almost next to the lake there's a little house where a gentleman called Harold Stainer lived with his sister. Harold was a renowned tailor and there's a famous photo of him sitting, cross-legged on a table, sewing. His sister was very involved with running the local Sunday school and was always respectfully addressed as Miss Stainer.

Harold Stainer sewing.

Jackie: We were much more aware of nature and the changing seasons back then. I'm sure we had snowier winters during our childhood. The snow was so deep we could walk on top of the hedges. The road to our cottage was little more than a track and we'd often be snowed in.

Jeanette: Snow days were special and our villages were often cut off from the rest of the world.

Jackie: I've got vague memories of the big freeze of 1962/63 and having to fetch bread and milk by sledge. With snow higher than the hedgerows for weeks on end it was no wonder the postman's van lay buried in Farm Hollow, an exposed village lane where snow drifted, for several weeks. Fortunately, the postie had managed to dig himself out.

Jackie's dad digging after heavy snow in 1978.

Jeanette: Signs of spring were very welcome after a hard winter, weren't they?

Jackie: Probably the first sign of winter's end in Compton was spotting snowdrops above the lane to Capstitch. Spring meant birdsong and pussy willow, daffodils, sticky buds and frog spawn. I always associate primroses with Mothering Sunday. Then bluebells appeared in shady woodlands. Fields and hedgerows were full of buttercups and daisies, forget-me-nots, ragged robin, violets, goose grass, elderflower and tiny wild strawberries.

Manor Farm, Compton was always known as Lewis's.

Jeanette: Nobody's allowed to pick wildflowers these days.

Jackie: 'Shroton Fair weather' was how my mum described the weather on a certain type of autumn day, when there was a nip in the air and the first mists of the season appeared. The annual fair at Shroton was held in September. Coles fun fair stands out in my memory and also the fact that it followed Shaftesbury carnival, another exciting autumn event.

Jeanette: Halloween wasn't really a 'big thing' back then was it? But Guy Fawkes Night was always celebrated.

Jackie: I think we always bought our own box of fireworks and built a bonfire with a Guy wearing an old pair of wellies, a flat cap and with a head made from a stocking stuffed with newspaper.

I loved looking in the box of fireworks, I think Standard was usually the make we bought and there was always a rocket, a Catherine wheel, a Roman candle and bangers. We had sparklers too. I loved the smell of the gunpowder and looking for the spent cartridges the next morning.

Jeanette: In Fontmell, it was usually the boys who went round the village collecting 'a penny for the Guy'.

Gourds Farm.

Jackie: Nowadays, people would think those boys were up to no good. But back then, it was an annual activity.

Jeanette: In the 60s, my uncle Arthur and aunty Joan ran The Crown Inn, the local pub in Fontmell, which was a hub of activity. And to one side of the pub is the old brewery, which in the early 70s was a pottery. In fact, I think it was part of Poole Pottery.

Jackie: And across the road from the pub was The Crown Garage, another thriving business, now long gone and replaced with housing.

Jeanette: These days there are far fewer really true locals living in Fontmell and the village of my youth is long gone. But I have happy childhood memories.

Jackie: I think we were very lucky to grow up during those decades. Life had been so very much harder for previous generations. Our grandfather William had left Compton to fight in the Great War. For North Dorset farm labourers in the 19th century, the only alternative was to answer the call from across the Atlantic where young men with a knowledge of agriculture were needed to help work the vast plains of the mid-west.

Jeanette: How very hard it must have been for our great great grandparents James and Elizabeth to say farewell to four of their sons when they left Compton in search of a better life in the USA in the late 19th century.

Jackie: Knowing they were unlikely to ever see those boys again. Our great grandfather sadly died in his early twenties so didn't 'go West' with his brothers.

Jeanette: But over the years, it's been good to meet the descendants of those Hardiman brothers when they've returned to Compton seeking out their roots.

Jackie: And it's good to be able to give them a snapshot of how village life was for previous generations.

2

Home Sweet Home

'…you might have a feature wall where the fireplace was and, like my Nan, three flying ducks on the wall...'

Imagine a house where …
There's no telephone.
There's no central heating or double glazing.
Homeware is functional, rather than decorative.
Automatic washing machines and fridges don't exist.

Jackie: Our first family home was at Capstitch in Compton, a brick and flint cottage which lay under the hill at the end of a no through lane. Looking back, it must have been pokey to say the least with a sitting room and open fire downstairs, a small kitchen with a Rayburn and a bathroom with a flat roof which had been 'tacked' on the side.

Capstitch Cottage, left, overlooked by Gourds Farmhouse.

Jeanette: We lived at 32 Orchard Close and later 20 Orchard Close, Fontmell. We moved there just after I was born in 1956. When I look back on things now, I realise how small our first little bungalow was. In the late 50s Orchard Close was a fairly new estate, inhabited mainly by families with young children at one end of the scale and at the other end, pensioners. As children, we always called it 'the circle'. It was a very friendly estate and everyone got on marvellously. Because Mum and Dad hadn't been married very long, they had very few items of value. This was still not long after the end of the war and so furnishings were very basic.

20 Orchard Close bedecked with frilly net curtains.

Baby Jeanette with brother David at 32 Orchard Close.

Jackie: We didn't have central heating. There was a paraffin heater on the landing to keep us warm overnight during the winter. My sister Sue's hot water bottle actually froze when it was left on a chair one very cold day. Ice often formed on the inside of the bedroom windows. The bathroom was so cold it was barely usable for bathing. As small children, we used a tin bath in front of the coal fire on Sunday nights. In fact, the only time the bath was regularly used was when Mum soaked Reverend Chaffey-Moore's white surplices, which she used to wash and iron.

Jeanette: I don't think we really felt the cold. We probably just put on another jumper.

Jackie: There was such a change in furniture during the 60s and 70s wasn't there?

Jeanette: In our sitting room there was a three-piece suite in green 'pleather', bought from Stratton's furnishers in Shaftesbury and in our 'best' room there was another suite in a sort of mustard coloured bouclé.

Jackie: My earliest memories of our sitting room are of the open coal fire with a tiled surround, brown leather suite, lino and rugs on the floor, a standard lamp with fringed shade and a small sideboard. In the kitchen there was a yellow and black Formica topped kitchen table with matching chairs that had white tubular legs, also bought from Stratton's in Shaftesbury. Apart from the Rayburn and the electric cooker there was no room for anything else in the small kitchen.

Jeanette: How about Granny Hardiman's home in Compton? She spent most of the time in the back living room didn't she? There was a Rayburn, two Staffordshire china dogs on top of the mantelpiece and a portrait of Queen Victoria hanging in the hallway.

The girls' grandparents' thatched cottage at Compton Abbas with cabbages all in a row.

Jackie: Yes, the 'front room' was kept for best. Uncle Jack would return from feeding the calves to have his breakfast of bacon and eggs washed down with a cup of Camp coffee. Gran's house always had an aroma of farmyard.

Jeanette: When you moved from Capstitch, didn't you live just across the field from Granny's house?

Jackie: Yes we did, from the late 60s. For just a few hundred pounds, my father bought a third of an acre from the landowner and built a bungalow called Greenacres which holds many memories for me. The views towards the airfield and the surrounding hills are stunning.

Jeanette: Of course, my dad, your mum and their eight siblings were brought up in Compton in a thatched cottage which lies a little further down the lane. At that time, thatched cottages were simple homes for the working classes. Nowadays they are undoubtedly extremely desirable and expensive properties.

Jackie: Our grandparents lived in that thatched cottage when I was a toddler and I have memories of Grandad sitting in a carver chair by the fireplace smoking a pipe.

Jeanette: Did Gran have any kitchen appliances?

Jackie: My earliest memory is the 'copper' in her scullery which was used every Monday washday. The 'copper' was a metal tub on legs and I helped her haul the boiling hot white sheets from it before passing them through a mangle that squeezed all the water from the clothes. There was always the danger of getting your fingers crushed in the rollers if you weren't nimble enough when feeding a bed sheet through.

Jeanette: In the 60s, my mum had a modern version of the 'copper' which was a square white tub with a mangle attached. I think it was made by Hoover.

Jackie: Then of course the twin tub came on the scene, which must have been such a relief for the woman of the house. There was a washing drum on the left and a spin dryer on the right. You still needed to be on hand though because when the wash was done the clothes had to be manually transferred to the spinner and woe betide if you didn't position them correctly or the machine made an almighty racket, vibrated violently and set off across the lino! There

Jackie still has her mum's Kenwood Chefette.

was also the excess water coming out of the back which needed to be routed via a pipe into the sink.

Jeanette: I think our first spin dryer was a Creda Debonair. We thought it was wonderful, but it was tiny and vibrated so violently it was like it had a life of its own!

Jackie: I think Mum and Dad bought white goods from E B Marsh, which is still going strong today.

Jeanette: I suppose in the days before the electrical superstore, we had to use local, family-run, businesses. There was a shop called Multi-Electrics at the bottom of the High Street in Shaftesbury.

Jackie: And the first fridges were under-counter size with a small ice box at the top which needed to be defrosted at regular intervals, which was a major event that entailed strategically placing bowls and towels on the floor to catch the melting water. When frozen food became popular, we had a huge chest freezer in the garage where all the fruit and veg, harvested from the garden, was stored.

Jeanette: In Fontmell, before buying a fridge we had a walk-in larder. And Nan Sims in Shaftesbury had something called a 'safe' where you kept things cool. It was simply a cupboard on the wall with chicken wire in the door.

Jackie: And quite often in the kitchen, instead of a blind, you'd probably have frilly net curtains tied back with a ribbon at the window.

Jeanette: Yes, but you'd also have some thicker curtains, with a matching frilly pelmet, which you'd close at night.

Jackie: Mum had a pressure cooker that scared me witless when it began to rattle and steam, but the contents were always delicious.

Jeanette: I know. The only cabbage I've ever enjoyed was cooked in my nan's pressure cooker.

Sunlight soap was used for scrubbing collars and cuffs.

Everyone had a mincer in their kitchen.

Jackie: Mum's electric carving knife was also well used, and I still use her little Kenwood Chefette hand mixer in my own kitchen.

Jeanette: And did you have some of those Tupperware containers in the kitchen?

Jackie: Oh yes, everyone had good old Tupperware. In fact, I think I've still got some.

Jeanette: Me too. It lasts for ever.

Jackie: What other gadgets did you have?

Jeanette still has Tupperware, a design classic.

Jeanette: We had one of those meat mincers that you screwed on to the edge of the table.

Jackie: I think we also had a 'state of the art' tea leaf dispenser on the wall. And one of those can openers that looked like a bull's head.

Jeanette: Our tea was always stored in a tin caddy with Chinese scenes on the outside.

Jackie: Did your mum use Sunlight Soap too?

The tea caddy.

Jeanette: She often used it to remove ground-in dirt from shirt collars. It was a massive bar of soap.

Jackie: I think Fairy was another well-known cleaning bar.

Jeanette: Wallpaper was very popular though, even in the kitchen where it would be wipeable. And in the lounge you'd probably have a feature wall over the fireplace and, like my Nan, three china ducks flying away somewhere.

Jeanette's maternal grandparents' home with three flying ducks on the wall.

Jackie: I often went with my dad, to the Colour Centre in Bell Street, Shaftesbury to pick up the huge wallpaper books before making a choice on wall coverings. Our kitchen wallpaper was adorned with images of rustic pots and pans in the 60s and in the 70s with orange geometric circles. The bathroom walls had seagulls framed against a light blue sky, which didn't help the cold room feel any warmer. Murals were also popular and Aunty Peggy had a huge, forest scene covering one wall in her sitting room.

Jeanette: Everyone had a sideboard in the sitting room, usually three drawers and couple of cupboards where the dinner service and best cutlery were kept, but seldom used. Glass cabinets were popular too, filled with lots of ornaments that nobody really ever touched.

Jackie: We had a radiogram with a turntable inside a huge teak cabinet with space inside for your LPs, old 45rpm and 78rpm vinyl records. In the 70s, wall units became the 'in thing' and ours also housed a cocktail cabinet alongside some popular ornaments of the time like the oversized red brandy glass, carriage clock with rotating balls and Spanish dancer doll brought back from an early package holiday.

Jeanette: We only had one bathroom, there was no such thing as an en suite in those days. Bathroom suite colours changed from plain white to pink, blue and avocado.

Jackie: We had some very funky clear blue plastic taps to match the bright blue bathroom suite.

Jeanette: Did you have a Teasmade? Great if you wanted a cuppa in bed, first thing in the morning. It saved boiling the kettle.

Jackie: Mum and Dad always used a Goblin Teasmade, but they still had to take the milk, water and tea leaves to bed with them, so you practically made the tea yourself.

Jeanette: It wasn't really until the 70s that furniture moved away from being purely functional to being more decorative. Fitted carpets replaced lino and usually had big, swirly patterns. Orange, brown and green featured heavily in the world of furnishings and every home also seemed to have a pouffé, usually in a leather effect fabric with a diamond pattern.

Jackie: Every sitting room also had an ashtray because most people smoked. There were hours of fun to be had pressing the button to make the ciggy disappear into the rotating ashtray on a stand.

Jeanette: But very few people had telephones in their houses; instead they used the one and only phone box in the village which in Fontmell was outside the village shop. In fact, like many of the lovely red phone boxes, it's still there, perfect for repurposing.

Quite often, there'd be a queue of people outside the telephone kiosk, all waiting to make a call and if you spent too much time in there, someone would knock on the window and order you to hurry up. It was also perfectly acceptable for someone to call you at the phone box.

The telephone box was a well used facility when few people had their own landline.

Jeanette: Yes, phone boxes were well used. And it must have been so annoying to be one of the few villagers who had a landline, because everyone else in the village frequently asked to use it.

Jackie: Our nearest box in Compton, at Twintown, was always kept spotlessly clean by Mrs Horlock who lived nearby. She'd regularly give it a good dust and polish.

But at Gourds Farm in Compton, where Mr and Mrs Harding lived and Mum worked, there was a cream-coloured phone which seemed the height of luxury.

Jeanette: In most houses, the telephone was in the hall on one of those telephone tables with the little padded seat and space for the directories. Our first phone number was Fontmell 777.

Jackie: Ours was Fontmell 673 and we'd say it every time we answered a call.

Jeanette: Yes, everyone always answered the phone by announcing their number. Nobody does that anymore.

3

Milk and Maypoles

*'I know one thing for sure Jackie. Mr Laycock was the most inspirational teacher
we ever had.'*

Imagine schooldays when…
Children can safely walk unaccompanied to and from the gates.
Lessons are often held in the headmaster's lounge.
Toilet tissue can 'double-up' as tracing paper.
There are no photocopiers or computers.

Jeanette: Of course, because I lived in Fontmell, it was a simple case of walking up the road to the primary school, but how did you get there Jackie?

Jackie: Well, when I was very little, Mum rode the two miles from Compton on her bike with me in a little metal chair on the back. No helmets or restraints in those days. But when I was older, I caught the bus.

Compton Abbas bus shelter.

33

Jeanette: I bet it was one of those buses with the prickly seats.

Jackie: That's right. I always caught the school bus from outside Compton Church. Then we'd get off the bus by the Crown Garage in Fontmell and cross the main road (with no help from a lollipop person), walk up the hill and on through the headmaster's garden towards the school building.

Jeanette: I can't imagine young children crossing that busy stretch of the A350 these days.

Jackie: I know. It sounds so dangerous. Although I suppose there was less traffic around in those days.

St Andrew's School, Fontmell today. The façade has changed little from the 60s.

Jeanette: Fontmell Primary took pupils from all the surrounding villages, Compton, Sutton Waldron, Bedchester, Twyford and others. And of course the headmaster, Douglas Laycock, lived in the adjoining schoolhouse with his wife (who taught the infants), and their four sons.

Jackie: Yes, they certainly lived and breathed school life.

Jeanette: We'd sometimes watch an educational TV programme in Mr and Mrs Laycock's lounge in the schoolhouse.

Jackie: It always seemed very dark in their lounge.

Jeanette: Probably because the curtains were drawn Jackie.

Jackie: Yes of course. But I can still picture their three-piece suite, which was black vinyl with yellow cushions.

Jeanette: Very swish. I know there was always a smell of coffee and cat food in their house. Strange what comes to mind.

Jackie: We'd also often listen to radio programmes. There was Singing Together and also Time and Tune. We had books to sing along with. We sang songs like 'He's Football Crazy' and 'John Brown's Body Lies A-mouldering In the Grave'.

Jeanette: I seem to recall 'Michael Finnegan' and 'Matthew, Mark, Luke and John'.

Jackie: Well, Mr Laycock is one of my all-time heroes.

Jeanette: He was a shortish, slim gentleman and always wore a three-piece suit and tie. He had jet-black hair, slicked back with Brylcreem hair grease. He always looked immaculate, not to mention handsome.

Jackie: Yes, I agree, he was very handsome, with lovely white teeth.

Jeanette: The school had three classrooms, didn't it? Infants with Mrs Laycock, middle with Mrs Young and senior (which we called 'big') with Mr Laycock.

Jackie: Mrs Young ran her class with a rod of iron, she didn't take any nonsense. She was probably only in her 40s, but to us youngsters, she seemed to be very old, probably because she had greying hair and wore glasses.

Jeanette: She surprised us all one summer by wearing a pair of mirrored sunglasses which I've never, ever forgotten. I'd never seen anything like them before.

Jackie: Every Wednesday, she'd teach all the older girls how to sew. We made stuffed animals out of felt and dressing table mats or handkerchief cases out of that strange 'holed' fabric called Binca that came in a range of colours and was ideal for practising cross stitch. I never knew it was called Binca at the time.

Jeanette: I still have a pin cushion that I made from pink felt and Binca. I gave it to my nan and when she died it came back to me. I think I also made a handkerchief case at some point, something that wouldn't be much use these days.

Jackie: Mrs Young taught us Maypole dancing too, which we'd perform at Fontmell village fete. We practised in the school playing field with the music blaring out from an old-style tape recorder (with two big reels) and amplified through a massive, wooden loudspeaker.

Jeanette: Every year the girls wore the same white tops and short, maroon skirts with elasticated waists and that wiggly Ric Rac ribbon sewn around the hem.

Jackie: You simply chose a skirt at random, it didn't matter which one you wore.

Jeanette: Talking of that playing field, I took a look at it recently and couldn't believe how tiny it seems now. I always thought it was massive.

Jackie: Funny how that happens isn't it? I guess we were so much smaller in those days.

Jeanette: And really strange how we did certain activities in the playground out front and other things in the playing field at the back.

Jackie: There were three parallel bars in the playground at the front weren't there? We dangled above the tarmac, never worrying about falling and fracturing our skulls!

Jeanette: No concerns about hurting ourselves in those days. We also did things like Music, Movement and Mime in the playground.

Jackie: That was a radio programme, wasn't it?

Jeanette: Yes. And we used equipment like plastic balls, hula hoops and those strange small, hard, rubber rings.

Jackie: Those rubber rings were like something you'd give to a dog.

Jeanette: We always wore plimsolls, not trainers. And they were black or white and either lace ups, or with a little elasticated insert at the front.

Jackie: I called those daps.

Jeanette: Really? I know my cousin Wendy from the Midlands called them pumps, which I thought was very strange. But white plimsolls had to be cleaned and kept white with that liquid whitener which needed to dry.

Jackie: Did we ever have a sports day at primary school?

Jeanette: I think so. But not one where parents were invited. We did things like the egg and spoon race, the sack race and the three-legged race. And we often did high-jump on the playing field plus we also had a long-jump pit. In fact, I competed in long-jump at the North Dorset Sports Day.

Jackie: Me too. And I also competed in both the relay and the 100 metres. I don't think I won anything though.

Jeanette: Sadly, I had three 'no jumps' and was disqualified. I was mortified.

Jackie: Oh, that's a shame. I'm not sure where that Sports Day took place. Was it Dorchester or Sturminster Newton?

Jeanette: Weymouth seems to ring a bell.

Jackie: We also played a lot of rounders, didn't we? Often against either Iwerne Minster or Ashmore Primary School. Ashmore was a tiny school, only about 10 pupils.

Jeanette: That's it. And the teacher was Miss Canavan. She drove a light-blue, Morris Minor and I think she used to fit most of the Ashmore school rounders' team in there.

Jackie: Of course, eventually, there was a swimming pool in the playing field at Fontmell School. One of those 'above-ground' ones.

The 'state of the art' swimming pool at Fontmell School - a fundraising campaign enabled its purchase.

Jeanette: Yes, there was a special fund set up to buy it and we indicated how much money had been saved on a big drawing of a barometer. It took months to save enough money. I mean, nowadays, most families simply buy one online and put it up in the garden. Back then it was a major purchase.

Jackie: Prior to that, we travelled up to Shaftesbury swimming pool every week.

Jeanette: On the public bus too. Imagine the teacher having to look after us all. It wouldn't be allowed nowadays.

Reading and writing competitions organised by Cadbury, Bourneville, Brooke Bond and Platignum were popular at Fontmell School. Jackie's 25-yard swim was achieved at Shaftesbury pool.

Jackie: I don't recall any football at primary school. There weren't any nets or goal posts set up anywhere. But I'm sure the boys would tell us were wrong.

Jeanette: The infants' classroom was fairly new.

Jackie: The infants sat at tiny tables with bags hanging from the back of the chairs containing all their books.

Jeanette: And Janet and John books were popular, often read aloud, standing at the teacher's desk.

Jackie: Just the sight of those cloth-covered books depicting Janet and John and I'm back there again.

Jeanette: At the rear of the infants' classroom there was a book corner and at the end of day, all the children sat, cross-legged on the floor and listened to teacher read a story. The books were stored in wooden, concertina-shaped shelves with a curtain wire keeping them in place.

Jackie: At lunchtime the infants' class doubled up as the canteen and at the back of the room there were bigger tables where the older children ate.

Jeanette: I always wanted to take a packed lunch. I hated school dinners.

Jackie: I always took a packed lunch when I was at primary school. There was a sandwich, probably filled with luncheon meat, which was very much like Spam, Smiths Crisps (with the little blue bag of salt) and a Penguin chocolate bar.

Jeanette: I was always quite jealous of all those kids with their little sandwiches, apples and chocolate bars. I'm convinced my hatred of boiled potatoes and gravy comes from those awful school dinners. The gravy was always lumpy and the spuds had black bits in them.

Jackie: But school lunches were really cheap, weren't they? Only about 2/6d (12.5p) per week.

Jeanette: That's why we had them.

Jackie: Mrs Westwood was the dinner lady. She wore a blue overall and was always very jolly. Two or three of the older girls helped to serve the food. We'd set everything up on trestle tables.

Jeanette: Mr Wills (although we called him Mr Wheels) delivered the lunches by coach. He lugged those massive, metal containers containing the food, through the playground.

Jackie: And we drank from those coloured metal jugs with matching metal beakers.

Jeanette: Mrs Laycock was my teacher in infants' class. She was a plump lady with dark curly hair, and she always smelt of Nivea.

Jackie and Jeanette's Fontmell School photos.

Miss Betty's infant class at Fontmell School.

Jackie: I was a couple of years below you and I was taught by Miss Betty, a really trendy lady who had first worked at the school as a student. She drove a light pink mini traveller van and wore very fashionable 60s clothes topped off with a blonde bob. We were all in awe of her and the fairy tale was completed later when she married Mrs Young's son. I still treasure a cutting about their wedding from the *Western Gazette*.

Jeanette: But we didn't have a uniform. So what did we wear to school?

Jackie: Lots of knitted cardigans and jumpers. Also, kilts were really popular, either with a bib, or with two straps, like braces.

Jeanette: And with a massive safety pin in the skirt. What about shoes? What did you wear?

Jackie: For school parties, I'd probably wear black patent shoes, with a strap across and little teardrop-shaped holes. But for everyday use, it was Go-Girls or maybe those shoes with the paw prints on the sole.

Jeanette: Those were called Wayfinders.

Jackie: You bought most school shoes from Frisby's in Shaftesbury, opposite the town hall.

Jeanette: You could get your feet measured there too.

Jackie: They sold Tuf children's shoes and also Clarks, both really popular brands.

Jeanette: And our PE kit hung in a cloth bag with string ties, on a peg in the cloakroom, with our name above.

Jackie: Yes, the PE kit was extremely basic, a vest, some shorts and plimsolls.

Jeanette: And the cloakroom toilets had that Izal, stiff toilet paper, rather like tracing paper, in square boxes on the wall. Not at all absorbent, everything slid off.

Jackie: I shudder to think about that awful stuff.

Jeanette: In Mr Laycock's class, for the first time, we had our own, big wooden desks with a sloping top and an inkwell. The ink monitor filled up the inkwells from a large bottle of Quink. Of course, there was a monitor for most tasks wasn't there? Blackboard monitor; book monitor; milk monitor.

Fontmell Magna C.E. School Class 2 Lower Juniors		July 1964
Subject	marks obtained	marks possible
Composition	8	10
Reading	9	10
Spelling	7	10
Arithmetic	16	20
Scripture	7	10
Geography	8	10
History	7	10
Nature Study	7	10
Art	8	10
	77	100

The Autumn Term begins on Wednesday 9th September

Jeanette's report from early days at Fontmell School.

Jackie: The milk arrived every morning in a crate. Each pupil was entitled to a third of a pint of milk which was drunk through paper straws during break. In winter, there was often ice on the milk and sometimes the birds beat us to it and pecked the silver foil tops.

Jeanette: The 'times-tables' were pinned up around the room and we learnt them in rote fashion which basically meant repeatedly chanting them.

Jackie: I can still recite all of them. Also, on one of the walls there was a really massive map of the world, with papier-mâché mountains painted in different colours.

Jeanette: Papier-mâché was very popular. Didn't we used to make it from newspaper and glue?

Jackie: That's right and it could be moulded into different shapes.

Jeanette: And of course, there was always a Nature Corner where we displayed things like leaves, flowers, stones and shells. We built it up throughout the term.

Jackie: It was such a treat to go for a Nature Walk. We picked lots of wild flowers and grasses, cowslips, primroses and violets. That's not allowed today of course.

Jeanette: In Mr Laycock's class we all entered annual competitions run by Cadbury and Brooke Bond. I recall winning quite a few of those contests.

Jackie: Me too. We had to write about making chocolate and the prize was usually a book token, although there was also a tin of chocolates, with a photo of Cadbury's headquarters in Bourneville on the lid.

Jeanette: I've never forgotten that Ghana used to be called the Gold Coast. And I loved that tin filled with chocolates. I used it as a pencil case for years after.

Of course, I also reached the dizzy heights of being head girl, with Nicholas Cuff as head boy. We were also Mary and Joseph in one of the Nativity plays.

Jackie: You sound like the Richard Burton and Elizabeth Taylor of Fontmell School.

Jeanette: Well, I suppose it was a bit like that.

Jackie: At Christmas, Mr Laycock used a piece of equipment called a Gestetner machine, an early form of photocopier, to print off our carol sheets. It involved turning a handle that produced the carol sheets in purple writing. The smell of methylated spirits comes back immediately.

Jeanette: I loved the end of the day, when we gathered around Mr Laycock and he read to us. Books like *101 Dalmatians*, *The Voyage of The Dawn Treader* and *The Lion, the Witch and The Wardrobe*.

Jackie: My favourite was *The Pilgrim's Progress*.

Jeanette: Really? I never liked that one. Far too long.

Jackie: I was sad to leave Fontmell Primary School. Weren't you?

Jeanette: I was quite sad, although I was excited about secondary school. Like many things, it's not until later in life that we realised what a wonderful school it was.

Jackie: When we left, we were each given a Holy Bible with an inscription inside the front cover, signed by Mr Laycock. I still have mine.

Jeanette and Jackie still have their battered Holy Bibles.

Jeanette: And I still have mine Jackie. It looks a bit worn.

Jackie: I'd recognise Mr Laycock's handwriting anywhere.

Jeanette: Yes, especially his signature.

Jackie: He was a legend.

Jeanette: I know one thing for sure, Jackie, without doubt he was the most inspirational teacher we ever had.

Jackie: I'll second that.

4

Sunday Best

'To this day, I still think of Gran Hardiman if I ever dare to use the washing machine on a Sunday.'

Imagine Sundays when…
Work or exertion of any kind is frowned upon.
Visits to or from relatives often take place.
No shops are open for trading.
Tea is a very special occasion.

Jackie: Gran Hardiman, who regularly attended chapel in Fontmell, didn't like anyone to do any chores, especially washing, on a Sunday. Because we lived just along the road from her in Compton, my mum wouldn't hang out the washing on a Sunday in case Gran spotted it! In fact, to this day, I still think of Gran Hardiman if I ever dare to use the washing machine on a Sunday.

Jeanette: I reckon Gran's beliefs rubbed off slightly on her children because my dad told me I wasn't allowed to wear jeans on a Sunday. He said they were far too scruffy, and it was disrespectful. He couldn't be swayed, even though he never seemed to be religious.

Jackie: Strange how our parents used to think. I always attended Sunday school in Compton Church and I've still got the album containing religious stamps that we collected each week.

Jeanette: For me, in Fontmell, aged about nine or 10 years old, the first port of call on Sunday was probably St Andrew's Church, where I was in the choir. As my parents weren't church-goers I suspect they sent me just to give themselves some peace and quiet for a couple of hours.

Jackie: Surely not, Jeanette.

Vestry where the choir prepared for services at Fontmell Church.

Jeanette: There was lots of giggling amongst us, particularly during the sermon when we'd become quite bored and fidgety. Eventually the vicar, Reverend Shorton, would pause in the pulpit, turn round and give us a stern look. That stopped us for a while… until the next time.

Jackie: Was the church busy back then, Jeanette?

Jeanette: Yes, it was always quite crowded and the same people always sat in the same pews. People dressed smartly for church with hats, ties and suits. I think it was a bit of a day out for some of them because, at the end of the service, most of them headed straight for the pub around the corner.

Jackie: Not a sin, I guess. But it shows you that they treated the church and the pub as a bit of a weekly meeting place. Somewhere to socialise.

The Methodist chapel at Fontmell.

St Andrew's Church Fontmell Magna.

Jeanette: Mind you, they weren't the only ones because Dad usually popped to The Crown in Fontmell for a pre-lunch pint on a Sunday and he always drank in the public bar, also known as the 'back bar'. That was where most of the locals gathered on Sundays.

Jackie: The lounge bar, known as the 'front bar' was reserved for more smartly dressed people, probably those who'd just arrived from church.

Jeanette: Dad had a pint, maybe played a game like bar billiards, shove-halfpenny or dominoes.

Jackie: We never see shove-halfpenny anymore. Didn't it involve sliding a coin along a board?

Jeanette: Yes, the board was quite shiny and your score depended on which area of the board you managed to land the coin. You used the side of your hand to shove it along the board.

Jackie: I think there was definitely a slight 'them and us' culture at Sunday lunchtimes, with the villagers in the public bar and 'the gentry' chatting together in the lounge bar, never mixing together.

Sunday drives often meant a stop off to feed the ducks at Ashmore pond.

Jeanette: True. But that's how it was back then. Anyway, Dad was on strict instructions to be back home in time for Sunday lunch.

Jackie: Yes, Sunday lunch was an important family occasion not to be missed.

Jeanette: In our house, Sunday lunch was always known as Sunday dinner, served at 12.30pm 'on the dot'. My mum started preparing the meal in the early morning, while she was doing her housework. Probably because she worked Monday through to Friday, Sunday was 'bedroom day' and the vacuum cleaner was in full swing for most of the morning, something which, as a teenager who liked to wallow in bed, annoyed me tremendously. I still hate the sound of a vacuum cleaner.

Jackie: We always had a Sunday roast with meat from one of the Shaftesbury butchers; Eastman's, Baxter's or Pike's. Mum bought chops, sausages, bacon, a joint for Sunday and, sometimes, pig's trotters and tripe for Dad. One thing's for certain, there was always a post-dinner discussion about the quality of the joint.

Jeanette: Whatever the meat, Mum smothered it in lard or maybe dripping which was stored in a cup after being strained. Everything had additional fat added to it, something that would be frowned upon these days.

Jackie: Nobody dreamt of eating out, especially on a Sunday. Things like carveries were unheard of. Also, these were 'pre-microwave' days and Mum cooked all the vegetables within an inch of their lives. Peas, beans, carrots, were all treated the same way, boiled in a saucepan till the colour had drained away.

We all sat around the table together as a family. And nobody ever dared leave the table without asking permission. That was one of the big positives about Sunday lunch; it was a time to eat together.

Jeanette: Around lunch time we listened to Family Favourites on the radio, probably, in the days before Radio One, on what was then called the Light Programme. I think that later that programme was renamed Two-Way Family Favourites and it connected families in the forces who were living in different countries.

Jackie: It was introduced by Jean Metcalfe and Cliff Michelmore, who met and married on the show, and later Judith Chalmers presented it.

Jeanette: Dad loved all those lunchtime farming programmes on TV. They weren't much like today's Countryfile. He often fell asleep in front of the TV, but if we dared to change the channel, he woke immediately and shouted 'I'm watching that'.

Jackie: We often visited relatives on a Sunday, always for tea, never lunch. Aunty Peggy in Blandford or Aunty Chris and Uncle Les in Parkstone. And we'd always take my sister Sue back to her lodgings in Poole where she was studying at college. Nowadays, people would simply commute to and from Poole daily but then it was normal to stay away for the week in lodgings, known as 'digs'. While we were there, we'd go down to Poole Quay and treat ourselves to a dish of cockles and mussels.

Jeanette's brother and cousins in 'Sunday Best'.

Jeanette: I often visited Gran Hardiman in Compton on a Sunday with Dad. Her house always smelt of home-made cake. I adored her fruit cake.

Jackie: She'd never have dreamt of buying a cake, or pickles for that matter. Everything was home-made or preserved.

Jeanette: Most people had a 'best room' to be used strictly for entertaining on special occasions, which meant it was hardly used at all.

Jackie: There had to be a 'best room'.

Jeanette: Our 'best room' had a yellow suite, teak sideboard, teak radiogram, plain green nylon carpet, fireplace feature wall covered in a patterned paper and the other three walls covered in plain paper, orange patterned curtains and frilly net curtains. I'm not sure how many times we actually sat in that room because we just passed through it on the way to somewhere else. It was always cold, hardly surprising as it was usually empty.

Jackie: And everyone had 'best' cutlery and china, quite often treasured wedding gifts. Those were the days when couples asked for a dinner service or a canteen of cutlery as a wedding gift which they would keep for life.

Jeanette: Our cutlery was always returned to the original box after use, and we had bone china teacups with a picture of a Japanese lady moulded into the bottom.

Jackie: 'Best' items were to be seen but seldom used.

The road past Springhead at Fontmell, a popular spot for a Sunday walk.

Jeanette: Sunday was also the day for a special tea and in our house it was often tinned pink salmon sandwiches, boiled eggs, Instant Whip or Angel Delight, tinned fruit, condensed milk and occasionally a block of ice cream bought from Mr Whippy's ice cream van, which dropped by every Sunday, playing a tune.

Jackie: Instant Whip and Angel Delight came in sachets in a variety of flavours didn't they? So delicious when whisked with cold milk. And ice cream was always packaged in thin cardboard, there were no plastic containers.

Jeanette: Without doubt, my favourite ice cream was Neapolitan (chocolate, strawberry and vanilla layers) although Raspberry Ripple was also very popular.

Jackie: At about 4pm we sat down to watch The Golden Shot. It had Bob Monkhouse and a lady called Ann Aston who was famous for being useless at adding up the scores.

Jeanette: That joke wore a bit thin after a time, but Bob kept on using it. It was a strange programme really, with a crossbow aimed at a target and contestants being blindfolded. And there was a famous line 'Bernie, the bolt please' whenever a bolt was loaded in the crossbow.

Jackie: There was always a Sunday serial especially for children at about 5.30pm.

Jeanette: I loved *Great Expectations* with Francesca Annis starring as Estelle. And *Anne of Green Gables* was another favourite.

Jackie: From 6pm there were religious programmes like 'Stars on Sunday' with Jess Yates at the organ and 'Songs of Praise', which is still going today. Then, at 7.25pm there'd be a regular Sunday evening drama series such as 'Howards Way' or 'The Onedin Line'.

Jeanette: I especially enjoyed *The Forsyte Saga*. Do you know, when the main character Soames eventually died it made front page news?

Jackie: Unbelievable. But in the evening there were programmes like 'Sunday Night at the London Palladium', introduced by Jimmy Tarbuck.

Jeanette: That was so popular and they had a quiz called 'Beat the Clock' plus a carousel where all the performers stood and rotated at the end of the show waving to the audience. I wasn't always allowed to stay up later than 9pm, so often didn't see this.

Jackie: Then there were other well-known programmes like 'Dr Finlay's Casebook', and 'Upstairs Downstairs' with an actor called John Quayle, who lived in Compton.

Jeanette: And all these programmes were in black and white. I don't think colour TV had arrived yet, certainly not in the 60s.

Jackie: On the radio, Pick of the Pops was an extremely popular radio programme. It was introduced by Alan 'Fluff' Freeman, and he ran through what was then called the 'Hit Parade', ending at 7pm with the current number one record.

Jeanette: He called the audience 'Pop-pickers'.

Jackie: And people often tried to record the show on blank cassette tapes, although it took a lot of patience trying to cut out the chat in between songs.

Jeanette: Yes, cassette tapes were rapidly taking the place of vinyl records.

Jackie: After Pick of the Pops, 'Sing Something Simple' came on the radio featuring The Cliff Adams Singers. Really boring for any teenager.

Jeanette: I hated that programme because when I was at school, it signalled the end of the weekend, time to have a bath and go to bed. I dreaded that 'Sunday Night' feeling.

Jackie: It's a shame really Jeanette; Sunday's no longer a special day, is it?

Jeanette: No. But it's quite funny that you still think of Gran Hardiman if you dare to hang out some washing.

Jackie's Sunday School sticker book.

5

Flowery Frocks and All That...

'Ladies in flowery dresses and white cardigans, the smell of freshly mown grass, the chink of cups and saucers and the rumble of the wooden ball on the skittle alley.'

Imagine an annual event that...
Evokes memories of warm summer days.
Attracts visitors from far and wide.
Unites the whole community.
Is a unique, English tradition.

Jeanette: Growing up in the 60s, the village fete was a major event, and most locals were there as well as visitors from the surrounding areas.

Jackie: It was a big day in the village calendar. My memories are of ladies in flowery dresses and white cardigans, the smell of freshly mown grass, the chink of cups and saucers and the rumble of the wooden ball on the skittle alley.

Jeanette: At Fontmell, the fete was always held at Fontmell House in Parsonage Street, which was a bit like the village manor house.

Jackie: Compton fete was held at the rectory, where Reverend Chaffey-Moore lived with his sister Mrs Faiers. There were terraced lawns with the tombola set up on the top terrace near the grand old house with more stalls on the lower lawns and a skittle alley at the bottom with straw bales arranged at the end to catch the wooden balls.

Jeanette: What was the tombola?

Jackie: It was a clear glass or plastic drum containing numbered tickets. People would pay to have a spin of the tombola drum and then pick out a ticket which would correspond to a prize.

'Crusaders' performed by Fontmell School pupils at Fontmell fete. Jackie, right, wearing crepe paper headgear.

Jeanette: I remember the rectory garden had sloping lawns.

Jackie: Yes. And one game that fascinated me involved a giant metal Slinky, which is a big spring really. I think we used to set it off down the slope with the aim of seeing who could get it to travel the farthest.

Handbell ringing at Compton fete.

The Rectory at Compton Abbas with its rolling lawns.
The venue for the village fete.

Jeanette: Ah yes, the Slinky builds momentum and moves along on its own. They were really popular when we were young.

Jackie: The ladies of the WI sold homemade cakes and served tea from a huge tea urn in proper cups and saucers. For children there might be orange squash, even lemon if we were lucky, or maybe an ice cream from a small mobile freezer. And of course, there were games, raffles and stalls selling all sorts of things.

Jeanette: I never quite understood why the white elephant stall was called the white elephant.

Jackie: Nor me. I think it was stuff that nobody wanted. I loved the Lucky Dip which was usually a basic dustbin filled with sawdust and covered in crêpe paper. We'd rummage for small parcels with a cheap toy inside, maybe a balsa wood glider kit, yoyo, some plasticine or a tiny baby doll.

Jeanette: Yes, such simple things. I loved guessing how many sweets were in the jar.

**Fontmell Magna
Village Fete**

№ 1626

GRAND DRAW

in aid of the Church, Chapel & Village Hall

First Prize £5

Prizes include

Wines, Chocolates, Cake, Chicken, Etc.

Draw to take place at Fontmell Magna Village Hall

on Saturday, 8th July 1972

Promoter: Mrs. B. Chick, "Fiferidge" Fontmell Magna

Registered under the Small Lotteries & Gaming Act, 1963

Ticket 2½p

1972 draw ticket from Fontmell fete.

Jackie: And because it was a special occasion we'd stay up late to hear one of the local groups such as The Ramblers.

Jeanette: Oh yes, they always made an appearance.

Jackie: And Fontmell fete would always hold a fancy-dress competition. Having a creative mum I was a regular entrant. I was a litter bin in the year of the national 'Take your litter home' campaign but my most memorable costume involved a silk kimono, a bun punctuated by knitting needles on my head and two blocks of wood from Dad's shed strapped to my feet. Being a geisha girl was not the most comfortable of outfits!

Jeanette: There was a girl in my class called Sally Ambridge who entered one year as a Spanish dancer. She wore a black lace mantilla and had real castanets. I was so jealous.

60

Fontmell School pupils performed The Pied Piper at the village fete.

Jackie: Fontmell Primary always put on a sort of short play with various themes. One year we did the Pied Piper of Hamelin. I was one of the rodents and James Strawbridge, wearing a cape and playing a recorder, took the lead role. Then, in the year of the Crusaders, I donned a knight's tabard and some huge crepe paper headgear.

Jeanette: And the children from Fontmell Primary School always entertained with some Maypole dancing. Off we went, weaving and then un-weaving the 'cobweb' around the wobbly white wooden Maypole.

Jackie: Yes, Maypole dancing was a big part of the fete.

Jeanette: Well, Jackie, even though it may not be quite so big and as important an event as it was back then, it's great that the village fete is still alive and kicking.

Jackie: It sure is, Jeanette.

'Flowery Frocks' worn by Jackie, her mum and sister Sue.

6

Coming Out to Play?

'...I didn't play with friends indoors; it was always outside.'

Imagine a childhood where...
Parents have no idea or worries about where their children are playing.
You can safely skip, walk or ride a bike in the middle of a road.
You spend hours building camps in the local wood.
Your local play area has just two swings.

Jeanette: It's probably unthinkable for parents of today, but for children growing up in the 60s, being allowed to wander here and there, unreachable, from dawn to dusk, was quite normal.

Jackie: I know, we thought nothing of it did we? As one of only a few children in Compton, I did the usual den building and exploring in the woods and surrounding hills. We spent many happy hours making camps under a fabulous ancient oak tree in the old walled churchyard at East Compton.

Jeanette: One of our favourite places in Fontmell was the wood known as Hatch Covert. If you look out across the field from the village hall to the left of West View, you can still see that wood. We made camps among the rhododendron bushes.

Jackie: Mobile phones were unheard of back then, so nobody could be contacted if anyone was injured or a problem arose. Parents expected to see us at mealtimes or bedtime but didn't worry in between.

Jeanette with dolly and on her trike at 32 Orchard Close.

Jeanette: In Fontmell, a big crowd of us children would often walk, maybe past Springhead and on up the road to The Higher Blandford Road, or perhaps to Bedchester. Nobody ever questioned where we were going or what time we were likely to return. We took the younger children in pushchairs; I don't think any adults came with us. Traffic was so much lighter then and there was no chance of being knocked over by passing cars. In fact, we walked in the middle of the road most of the time.

Fontmell play park was opened in the 60s.

Jackie with her dolls.

Jackie: Yes, some days we walked to the local chalk pit to search for fossils and well-shaped pieces of chalk which we used for hopscotch.

Jeanette: I loved hopscotch. We'd scrawl numbers one to ten on the pavement and play for hours.

Jackie: Yes. We were always chalking over the pavements and roads. Nobody thought anything of it.

Dangerous activities like attaching ropes to high tree branches, swinging over tarmac, climbing trees, using penknives, and hurtling downhill in homemade go-karts were all part of everyday play.

Jeanette: Not forgetting kiss chase.

Jackie: We didn't have enough boys in Compton for kiss chase.

Jeanette: That's a shame. So exciting being caught by your favourite boy and having a quick snog. Thrilling.

Jackie: But I never played with my mates indoors; it was always outside. And friends knocked the door and asked if you were 'coming out to play'.

Jeanette: Games like skipping with a rope stretched across the road with two or three jumping together were popular. We often played in the street.

Jackie: And we rode our bikes most places. Bikes would simply be abandoned anywhere. Not a padlock in sight.

Jeanette: Yes, when I was very small my dad taught me to ride my bike by letting go without me noticing. I progressed from Triang tricycles and scooters to Raleigh bikes.

Jackie: Sadly, we only had two swings outside the village hall in Compton. Not much of a play park.

Jeanette: It was slightly better in Fontmell. Outside the village hall, there were two sets of swings set in concrete and two parallel bars. We spent endless hours down there on those swings, rising as high as we could into the air, surrounded by nothing more than glorious green fields, trees and hills.

Jackie: We simply made our own entertainment and had such great fun together.

'Dressing up' was a popular pastime for the village children in Compton.

Jeanette: But if we had to stay indoors, dressing up was always popular.

Jackie: Our dressing up box contained cast-offs from the 'big house' up the road in Compton. Lacy ballgowns, 1930s flapper dresses, hats and fans and, my favourite, a real fox fur stole with fox's snout which clipped to its tail. Unthinkable today.

But we also played the usual board games like snakes and ladders, ludo, draughts and card games such as rummy and beat jack out of doors.

Jeanette: And paper dollies came with a whole wardrobe of paper clothes and accessories that could be attached with tiny tabs. The back page of the *Bunty* comic always had extra clothes to dress your dolly in.

Jackie: I loved real dollies and had a big collection including 'Millie' a dolly which, after losing her hair and one arm, Mum painstakingly rebuilt, gluing rabbit fur to her head and replacing her upper limb.

Jeanette: So funny how we can still remember the names of our favourite dolls isn't it?

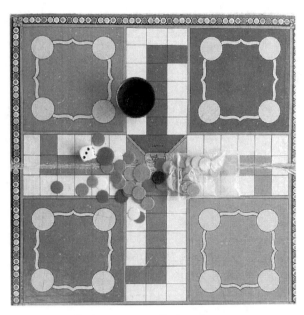

Ludo was a popular board game.

Jackie: One memorable toy from the 60s is my Sindy doll, which I still have. She's wearing her denim pedal pushers and tennis pumps. Sindy's boyfriend Paul, who lives in the memory box with her, is starting to look a little dated in his 'motoring' outfit of sheepskin coat, check trews, black turtleneck, and Chelsea boots. But after all these years he still has his tiny Thermos flask.

Jeanette: I really wanted a Tressy doll with hair that grew, so my aunties clubbed together and bought me one from Bridles, the toy shop in Shaftesbury High Street. I think she cost twelve shillings (60p).

Jackie: Sooty and Sweep were also an early favourite of mine after I inherited the straw stuffed puppets from 'the big house'. I even went to see them 'live' at a show on Bournemouth Pier although they wouldn't have travelled far because in real life they lived with their 'minder' Harry Corbett in nearby Child Okeford.

Jeanette: I've got a vivid memory of driving past his house in Child Okeford and seeing the Sooty and Sweep statues on the gate posts.

Jackie playing nurse in the garden at Capstitch Cottage, Compton.

Jackie: Another early 'toy' memory is when I was four years old, my older sister Sue and I were given a big wooden box of Lego for Christmas. My grandchildren still play with it, which is a tribute to Lego's amazing longevity.

Jeanette: Lego's one of the few toys that's stood the test of time.

Jackie: We also played 'cat's cradle', winding pieces of elastic into intricate webs through our fingers and 'jacks', using a small rubber ball and metal crosses.

Jeanette: I can't imagine today's children will cherish their first toys in the same special way that we did.

Jackie: Well, I suppose it's easy to look back with rose-tinted specs at what some might see as an idyllic childhood when, in reality, there were many days when we were bored out of our minds.

Everyone had Snakes and Ladders in the 60s.

Playing on the garden 'furniture' circa 1960
with Janet the doll and Smokey the cat.

7

On Our Doorsteps

'Everything was cooked in lard. Olive oil was only found in the local chemist.'

Imagine a time when…
Most everyday staples are delivered to the door.
Supper is one of the main meals of the day.
A full English breakfast is cooked in lard.
Frozen food is a thing of the future.

Jackie: Having your groceries delivered has become popular again. Were there food deliveries when we were growing up, Jeanette?

Jeanette: Yes, there were. In Shaftesbury Nan Sims would drop her weekly grocery order into International Stores and there was a set day when they'd be delivered. When not everyone had a car, delivery men were a common sight.

Jackie: Although Compton village shop closed many years ago, the former shopkeeper, Mr Ellingham, made deliveries around the village in his Morris Traveller. Groceries were packed in cardboard boxes. There were no plastic carriers at all.

Jeanette: Yes, the village shop was a well-used amenity in the 60s and 70s.

Jackie: Certainly most people had milk delivered to their doorstep in glass bottles. You left a note, instructing how many pints you wanted. Some people had those little crates with a dial to indicate how many bottles were needed.

Jeanette: And Mum thought nothing of leaving money outside in an envelope to pay the milk bill.

Corona came in every flavour under the sun.

Jackie: The 'bread man' Victor came in his little van from Ottons in Iwerne Minster with fresh bread and cakes.

Jeanette: Victor had such a deep voice, but he was very jolly.

Jackie: I was allowed to go out to choose a cake from the back of his van. He'd slide out the huge wooden trays and I'd usually settle for a jam and cream horn or a chocolate éclair.

Jeanette: I liked those puff pastries called 'traffic lights' with three different flavours of jam.

Jackie: Mum often bought a bloomer or cottage loaf; I don't think there was any sliced bread. Everyone sliced their own.

Jeanette: Every home had a bread board and bread knife.

Jackie: I think the first sliced bread, which was thin, white and gluey, was Mother's Pride. The thick cut came in a blue and white waxed wrapper and the medium cut in a red and white wrapper.

Jeanette: And when brown bread began to appear, it was thought of as quite radical. I think Hovis was the first.

Fontmell Post Office and Stores.

Jackie: Another daily visitor was 'the paper man' Mr White from Shroton. Mum and Dad had the *Western Gazette* delivered every week; this was when it was broadsheet size. I also had my comic delivered by the paper man and looked forward to reading the latest *Teddy Bear* or *Jack and Jill* before moving on to *Twinkle, Diana* and *Jackie.*

Les and Glynis Barrett in Fontmell village shop in the 70s.

The paper man always gave our dog a biscuit after he'd popped our newspaper in the drainpipe, always wedged in the hedge, from where we collected it.

Jeanette: The *Western Gazette* contained everything about the area didn't it?

Jackie: Oh my goodness yes. Marriages, deaths, births, adverts, house sales…you name it. Most people read it every week.

Jeanette: We also had an oil man who brought paraffin for our little stove. And the coalman, from Hayters in Shaftesbury, was another regular visitor.

Jackie: The coalmen always wore donkey jackets and caps and were covered in black coal dust from head to toe. They hauled those hessian sacks of coal on their backs from the flatbed lorry to the coal bunker.

Jeanette: They must have all ended up with back injuries Jackie.

Jackie: Yes, those sacks were so heavy.

Jeanette: There was also a fish and chip van that called regularly, although we often popped to Shaftesbury for chips, either to Gray's in Bell Street or Stretch's in Coppice Street. Fish and chips were always wrapped in real newspaper and it was a big treat. You could get a sixpenny bag of chips and ask for scraps.

Jackie: Apart from fish and chips, we didn't have any takeaway food, did we? My first taste of more exotic foods were the Vesta ready meals. I loved the beef risotto, little packets of dried and processed rice, beef and veg which you brought to life, Pot Noodle style, with hot water.

Jeanette: I always wanted the Kelloggs variety packs, but Mum said that was a waste of money as I wouldn't like all of them. Breakfast cereals often contained a free toy, usually part of a set which you could collect.

Jackie: I loved delving into the cereal box to fish out a plastic figure; cowboys and Indians in the Rice Krispies and 3D viewing cards in the Weetabix packets. You had to send off for the little red viewing glasses which I still have.

3D viewing glasses and sets of viewing cards.

Jeanette: My dad often had Shredded Wheat for breakfast. I could never understand the attraction. It tasted like straw to me.

Jackie: My dad usually enjoyed a full English breakfast and gave me delicious forkfuls of fried bread dipped in sticky free range egg yolk. Of course, everything was cooked in lard. Olive oil was only found in the local chemist. The first cooking oil we had was Krisp 'n' Dry in the 70s.

Jeanette: But generally, it was all fresh ingredients although frozen food became more popular in the 70s. I loved Brain's Faggots.

Jackie: My frozen favourites were Birds Eye peas, fish fingers and Arctic roll.

Jeanette: We always had supper, even if it was only bread and cheese. Dad often had pilchards with bread and butter.

Jackie: We didn't snack between meals at all and if we did have something like a biscuit, we'd only ever be allowed one or two.

Jeanette: Three square meals a day was obviously much better for our health. I think we were so lucky to have grown up with proper home-cooked food.

8

Pub Life

'...you knew almost everyone. It was a place for everyone to congregate, play cards, darts, bar billiards, shove halfpenny and other games, particularly at weekends.'

Imagine a pub where…
Everyone dresses smartly on Saturday nights.
Most patrons routinely drink and drive.
Smoking is totally acceptable.
Meals aren't available.

The Crown Inn at Fontmell.

Jackie: I think The Crown in Fontmell was my first experience of a pub because we didn't have a pub in Compton, so my dad always drank there.

Jeanette: Did he used to walk from Compton to Fontmell?

Jackie: No. In the days before drinking and driving became an offence, people from Bedchester, Twyford and all the surrounding villages visited The Crown, drank all evening and drove home. I don't think the breathalyser was introduced until the late 60s.

Jeanette: And even when it was introduced, I don't think it made much difference to anyone in the villages did it?

Jackie: No, everyone carried on as before. Didn't your aunty and uncle run The Crown?

Jeanette: Yes, they did. And they were famed for their legendary 'lock-ins'.

Jackie: What's a 'lock-in'?

Jeanette: After the pub closed at about 10.30pm, they'd lock the doors, continue serving drinks, have a bit of a party and a game of spoof, a strange game where everyone hides coins in their fists, and you have to guess the total number of coins in the group. It gave everyone endless hours of amusement.

Jackie: What were the official business times?

Jeanette: They were more restricted than nowadays. Monday to Saturday, the pub opened at lunchtimes, closed at 2pm and then reopened from 6pm to 10.30pm. On Sundays, the pub opened midday to 2pm and then reopened at 7pm. And during the summer when haymaking was underway, the pub stayed open until 11pm so the farm labourers could grab a late drink.

Jackie: So quite a commitment.

Jeanette: Yes, but Joan and Arthur were also quite well known for over-sleeping and opening the pub late. It was quite normal to see someone hammering on the door, demanding that the pub be opened. I think it's pretty fair to say that Arthur and Joan were often late risers.

Uncle Arthur and Aunty Joan behind the bar at The Crown Inn, Fontmell.

Jackie: The pub was an important part of the village, wasn't it? Full of locals.

Jeanette: It certainly was and if you walked in, you knew almost everyone. It was a place for people to congregate, play cards, darts and other games, particularly at weekends.

Jackie: Fridays were usually Thrift Club evenings when people dropped in, paid their contribution to the club, and checked in with everyone else. Thrift Clubs were popular in the 60s and 70s and were a good way of putting away a little money as and when it became available.

Jeanette: The big pay out was at Christmas, in good time for buying the turkey and gifts.

Jackie: There were always two bars weren't there?

Jeanette: Yes, the public bar was more casual and men in work clothes were allowed to drink there. But the front bar, known as the saloon or lounge, was posher and certainly my dad only went in there at weekends when he was dressed smartly.

Jackie: I know my dad went to the pub on a Saturday nights. And he dressed up smartly too. Nothing casual in those days; certainly no jeans. He washed and shaved beforehand, put on a clean shirt and tie and if not a suit, it was a smart blazer or sports jacket and trousers.

Jeanette: My dad often left the house with small pieces of tissue paper all over his face where he'd cut himself shaving. Hopefully he removed them before he got to the pub.

Saturday night was the 'big' night out when he sat in the lounge bar. He always had his playing cards, his cribbage board and his darts. He also played in the local darts league during the week. It was all about meeting your mates, having a game of cards, a few pints and a smoke.

Jackie: There was always a 'fruit machine' or 'one-armed bandit' in the pub. Pretty simple though, all you had to do was get three lemons, cherries or plums in a row and you probably got the jackpot. I think you bought special tokens from behind the bar to use in the machine.

Jeanette: There was also a juke box in the front bar of The Crown. They were fairly common in the 60s. I think you inserted something like 6d and pressed buttons like A1, B2 to select the tune of your choice, all vinyl records of course.

Jackie: The other thing The Crown was well-known for was its toilets, which were literally over the other side of the stream. If there were strangers in the pub who asked directions to the toilet, you sent them through the back bar and over the bridge. Of course, they often thought it was some kind of practical joke.

Jeanette: Unlike today, there were no meals served in the pub. Early in the 70s Aunty Joan started making toasted sandwiches, but until then, it was simply a bag of crisps, maybe some peanuts or a bar of chocolate.

Jackie: Probably Smith's crisps, with the little blue salt bag. And maybe you'd spoil yourself by having a pickled egg with them.

Jeanette: That's still a big favourite with me, Jackie.

The Mitre Inn

Tel.: Shaftesbury 2488
(3142 Guests)

Station: Gillingham

An Old Inn, modernised, having panoramic views of North Dorset and the Blackmore Vale, whilst situated in the centre of the town

Your Hosts—
Mike and Petronella Davis-Sellick

Traditional Home Cooking—Buffet Bar—Fully Licensed—Hot and Cold water in all Bedrooms—Central Heating—Old-world Hospitality combined with all modern comforts—T.V. in Bedrooms—Parking and Lock-up Garages

Jackie: I think the first pubs I visited for food were The Mitre in Shaftesbury, who did a cracking 'chicken in a basket' and The Plough at Manston.

Jeanette: 'Basket' meals were certainly all the rage. And places like The Plough served up a good steak and chips.

Jackie: Everyone smoked. The bar was shrouded in a haze of smoke with massive ceramic ash trays, or those little tin ash trays all around the place. Nobody gave a second thought to the dreadful smell, the passive smoking or any of the health hazards. Smoking was perfectly acceptable, along with nicotine-stained walls and ceilings.

Jeanette: But there were no cigarette machines in the 60s and 70s. The pub stocked a small selection of cigarettes, No6, No10 and Embassy. And there were very few disposable lighters. Most people had their own metal lighter, or used matches that were often given away free at the pub and came on a tiny piece of card. In fact, I collected matchboxes at one point.

Jackie: Lots of customers had their own drinking tankard, often pewter, which they left in the pub. The tankards hung above the bar and the person serving knew which customers had their own mug.

Jeanette: Saturday night was also the night for a pub crawl. And although Dad frequently ended up having a final pint at The Crown, he often drove elsewhere to pubs such as The Listen Inn at Cann, or maybe The Two Brewers in St James. I can still clearly see the sign for The Listen Inn which was an enormous hand cupping an ear.

Jackie: I think a woman called Mrs Archer was landlady at The Listen Inn.

Jeanette: Also, on Saturday, Dad often took my grandad with him to the pub. I can see Grandad now, standing in front of the fire at 17A Gold Hill, dressed in his 'best' blazer, which had an embroidered yellow military badge on the pocket, clean shirt, neat tie and pressed trousers. But most of all, I can see his shoes, which he had polished to a brilliant shine. And he'd keep asking me if they were shiny enough, knowing full well they were perfect. Looking back now, I can still feel his excitement at the prospect of going for a drink, smoking to his heart's content and meeting up with all his friends. Saturday nights were a real occasion for him.

Jackie: All pubs were adult spaces then though, nobody dreamt of taking children to the pub.

Jeanette: It was taboo for kids. But generally, pubs had a small window, usually situated at the side of the bar, where people bought alcohol, lemonade or returned empty bottles. This was known as the off licence or the 'offy' and children, who were not allowed in the main bar, could use it. Also, frequently when we were out in the car for a weekend drive, Dad would stop, park up in a pub, go for a pint and bring crisps and lemonade on a tray out to us sitting in the car. There was something special about that.

Jackie: Of course, you couldn't buy alcohol in the supermarket.

Jeanette: No. Which was why most people went to the pub for a drink and a night out. It was a social occasion.

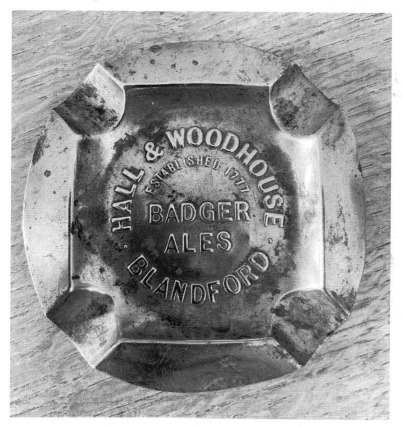

Every pub in the 60s and 70s had a variety of ashtrays.

Jeanette: What was your first 'grown-up' drink?

Jackie: Probably Babycham. Because that was like the alcopop of its day, wasn't it?

Jeanette and brother David at The Crown at Fontmell circa 1970s.

Jeanette: The advert used to say 'Babycham, sparkling champagne perry'.

Jackie: What about you? What was your first alcoholic drink?

Jeanette: I think probably Cinzano and lemonade. Then I moved on to dry Martini and lemonade.

Jackie: Very posh.

Jeanette: Then I think it was gin and orange. But it was always orange squash, not juice. Why didn't we drink juice?

Jackie: Goodness knows. I mean, I used to drink vodka and lime cordial. How sickly must that have been?

Jeanette: Nobody drank wine, did they? Certainly, it was unheard of in pubs.

Jackie: Probably into the 70s you could buy Liebfraumilch or Blue Nun. They were really sweet white wines. Or Mateus Rosé, which came in those lovely bottles with straw bases which everyone made into table lamps.

Jeanette: Lovely lamps. I think people only bought the wine for the bottle.

Jackie: Well, all I can say Jeanette is…cheers!

9

A Spoonful of Sugar...

'I always thought it was odd that even though he was a very tall man, Dr Tapper drove a little Mini!'

Imagine a Health Service where...
You can phone the surgery at any time to make an appointment.
Doctors routinely do their 'rounds' and make house calls.
There's a strong smell of disinfectant in the Hospital.
You have a dedicated family doctor.

Jackie: Medical services have changed since we were children.

Jackie and Jeanette were born at Shaftesbury's Castle Hill House when it was a maternity hospital.

Jeanette: They certainly have. We knew our family doctor from birth. I was born at Castle Hill House in Shaftesbury when it was the local maternity hospital.

Jackie: Me too. It's such a lovely old house. Do you know which doctor delivered you?

Baby Jeanette came home from Castle Hill House maternity hospital to 32 Orchard Close in Fontmell.

Jeanette: I think it was a Dr Lees, but I know that growing up, our family doctor was Dr Tapper.

Jackie: Gran Hardiman knew Dr Tapper well because she attended the chapel at Fontmell and Dr Tapper was a Methodist lay preacher. He came out to see me when I had various childhood illnesses, but our family doctor was Dr Chapman and then, later on, Dr Jones.

Jeanette: I always thought it was odd that even though he was a very tall man, Dr Tapper drove a little Mini! And he always had a pen sticking out of his mouth.

Jackie: I can see him now rushing into the house in his tweed jacket carrying his big leather doctor's bag, not very commonplace today. We always went to the garden fete which was held at his home The Mount in Shaftesbury.

My other, rather bizarre, memory of Dr Tapper is him telling my Mum it was good for children to run about in bare feet.

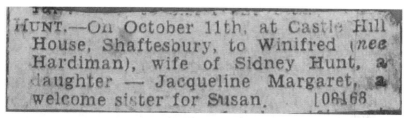

HUNT.—On October 11th, at Castle Hill House, Shaftesbury, to Winifred (nee Hardiman), wife of Sidney Hunt, a daughter — Jacqueline Margaret, a welcome sister for Susan.

Births were usually announced in the Western Gazette.

Jackie (with cousin Heather) came home to Capstitch Cottage from Castle Hill House maternity hospital. The pram wheels were subsequently used on a go-cart.

Jeanette: Dr Powell made regular visits to my grandparents when they lived on Gold Hill, often just to see how they were. Unheard of nowadays. He was a very well-respected GP.

Jackie: Shaftesbury surgery was at Barton Hill in a bungalow that's still there today. Then, in the 70s, they built the new, bigger Health Centre in Bimport.

Jeanette: Yes, and if you had an appointment, you always spotted someone you knew in the waiting room and wondered why they were there. Making an appointment was easy then though, you just picked up the phone and asked to see your own doctor who not only knew all your medical history but all your family's too. There was also a surgery held in the chapel at Fontmell.

Jackie: All the prescriptions were handwritten, and it was only the chemist who could read the doctor's handwriting. Tablets came in little brown glass bottles with a bit of cotton wool in the neck and there were no safety caps. We wouldn't dream of heading to the pharmacist for minor ailments like we do today. They were there simply to make up your prescription.

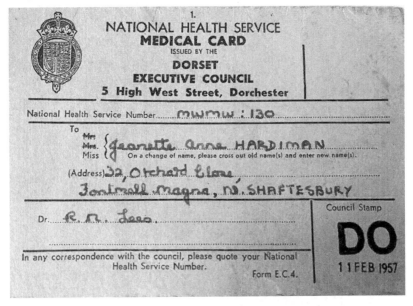

Jeanette's medical card from the time when healthcare was straightforward.

Jeanette: We had certain health checks and inoculations at school. Certainly at Fontmell School we were given a sugar cube for polio. At Shaftesbury High School we had the BCG, for TB, which left a mark on our upper arms. I don't recall our parents ever being asked to give permission for any of the vaccinations, which is odd.

Jackie: No, I don't think we took a slip home to get permission. Of course, there's so much which was allowed in the 60s which is frowned upon today. Teachers could give us an aspirin or a Disprin for a headache. Everything's so regulated now, even the first aid box.

Jeanette: It was quite nice to be off school and be spoilt at home though, wasn't it?

Jackie: Oh yes, I loved being able to lie on the sofa and watch TV, even though there were very often only educational programmes on during the day. Mum often bought a bottle of Ribena or Lucozade. I have no idea why Lucozade was wrapped in orange cellophane, but it was a real treat. Meals, often soup, were presented on a tray and Mum would bring a bowl and flannel to mop my fevered brow. I think bed rest was seen as very important back then.

Jeanette: Mum made fresh orange juice for me. And Nan Sims swore by something called Dr Collis's which she thought could heal anything and everything. Calamine lotion was used for any rashes.

Jackie: Calamine was really cooling when you had itchy spots but was quite uncomfortable when it dried on your skin. I'm sure Mum gave us bicarbonate of soda when we had an upset tummy or Milk of Magnesia.

Jeanette: And Andrews Liver Salts for indigestion.

Jackie: Did you have your tonsils out as a child? Everybody seemed to. I had mine taken out, with my adenoids, when I was five. I think I was in Odstock Hospital, now called Salisbury District Hospital, for about a week. In fact, people actually sent me postcards while I was in there and I've still got them.

Jeanette: Well, there was no option for parents to stay so you were on your own in a children's ward.

MEDICAL SERVICES

General Medical Practices:

Dr. W. M. Chapman, Tel. 2519 — Surgery Hours:
Dr. F. J. Powell, Tel. 2553 — The Surgery, Barton Hill
Dr. G. W. Tapper, Tel. 2747 — Shaftesbury. Tel. 2371
Dr. John Trowell, Tel. 2173 — 9 a.m.—12.30 p.m.
2 p.m.—7 p.m.

In case of emergency, telephone the Surgery, or an individual doctor at his residence when Surgery is closed.

Dental Surgeons:

Mr. R. W. Pinniger, Avis Hayes, Shaftesbury. Tel. 2497
Mr. R. G. Carnall, Avis Hayes, Shaftesbury. Tel. 2497
Mr. J. H. Gibson-Smith, 1, Iona, Victoria Street, Shaftesbury. Tel. 2255
Mr. Philip Maynard, School Dental Service, Dental Clinic, Modern School, Shaftesbury. Tel. 2852
Home: Sweets House, Stour Row. Tel. East Stour 201

County Medical Officer of Health:

Dr. A. F. Turner, County Hall, Dorchester. Tel. Dorchester 1000.

Medical Officer of Health for North Dorset:

Dr. Noel F. Pearson, County Offices, Sturminster Newton. Tel. Stur. Newton 636.

Infant Welfare Clinic: Held at the Modern School, Shaftesbury, first and third Tuesdays in the month, 2 p.m.— 4 p.m.

Health Visitor:

District Nurse and Midwife:

Mrs. V. Glaze, 12, Barton Hill, Shaftesbury. Tel. 2962.

District Welfare Officer:

Miss V. D. Gould, Home Address: Middle Cottage, Melbury, Shaftesbury. Tel. 2539.
Office Address: The Clinic, 57 Green Close, Sturminster Newton. Tel. Stur. Newton 652.

Comprehensive medical services available in the 60s in the Shaftesbury area.

90

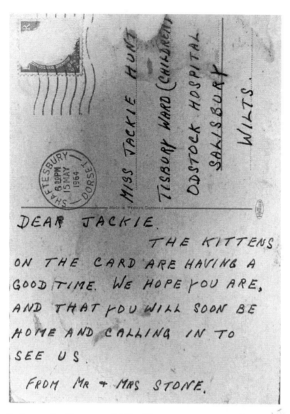

The following is written on the postcard:

MISS JACKIE HUNT
TISBURY WARD (CHILDREN)
ODSTOCK HOSPITAL
SALISBURY
WILTS

DEAR JACKIE.
THE KITTENS
ON THE CARD ARE HAVING A
GOOD TIME. WE HOPE YOU ARE,
AND THAT YOU WILL SOON BE
HOME AND CALLING IN TO
SEE US.
FROM MR + MRS STONE.

A hospital stay for five year old Jackie meant corresponding by postcard.

Jackie: I loved the jelly and ice cream. The little girl in the bed next to me had a lovely blue candlewick dressing gown which I coveted.

Jeanette: That's such a strange thing to remember, Jackie. I had my tonsils out when I was 11 and I loved being in the hospital, especially when the tea trolley with comics and books came around.

We both stayed in Odstock but of course Shaftesbury's Westminster Hospital had a proper A&E. Aunty Jean worked there in the 60s and she often talked about the matron and how everything had to be kept immaculate or there'd be trouble. Hospitals always smelt so strongly of disinfectant then.

Jackie: I think I went to Shaftesbury hospital when I twisted my ankle in the playground at Fontmell School.

Jeanette: I went there with a poisoned finger. That taught me never to bite my nails again! I think they gave me gas and air when it was treated. Whatever it was, I kept smelling it for months after.

Jackie: Well, Castle Hill House became a care home at one time, didn't it?

Jeanette: Yes, and then it closed. But we could well have ended our days in the same place we were born.

Jackie: It was hardly the Exotic Marigold Hotel, but hey, it could have been fun.

10

Baby You Can Drive My Car

'We swam in the sea, watched Punch and Judy, built sandcastles and went on the donkey rides…'

Imagine driving when…
Ashtrays and cigarette lighters are routinely fitted in cars.
You take all your own food and drink on family outings.
You plan your route using an Ordnance Survey map.
Most households have just one family car.

Jeanette: Our first family vehicle was a motorbike and sidecar.

Jackie: I think that was our very first vehicle too. They were really common when we were young.

Jeanette: Mum rode pillion behind Dad and my brother David and I were snug inside the sidecar.

Jackie: Apparently my dad once drove 400 miles on his motorbike to visit relatives in South Shields and Mum, several months pregnant, travelled in the sidecar.

Jeanette: Amazing but slightly scary. Anyway, eventually we moved a bit upmarket, and Dad got an old black Morris. He often used a starting handle to get it up and running. He inserted it in the front grill and wound it round and round till the engine got going.

Jackie's dad's Morris van.

Jackie: We had something similar. An old black Austin, I think. Most cars were black, and all cars had those yellow indicators that flipped out from either side of the car.

Jeanette: I think our first 'newish' car was a white Thames van. Dad put an old coach seat in the back where we children sat. One day, we were returning from the beach and some of my friends were in the van. One of the wheels fell off and we found ourselves scraping and screeching along the road. It must have been quite scary for all of us, but as children you simply take it in your stride. It was a memory we often recalled as we grew up. We certainly never let Dad forget it.

Jackie: Oh no. That's really frightening. Eventually, our family moved on to a Hillman Husky, registration PFX 33. So funny how I can still recall the registration number.

Jeanette: Isn't it strange? But likewise, our first brand new car was a sky-blue Ford Anglia, registration CTK 455C.

I'm really not sure how Mum and Dad afforded a brand-new car because they always flatly refused to buy anything on credit. But I know there was great excitement about visiting the garage and choosing the colour.

Jackie's dad and his Hillman Husky.

Jackie: I think the two most popular cars on the road at that time were probably the Ford Anglia and the Ford Cortina.

Jeanette: The Cortina had unusual back lights, a circle split into three sections, very swish. And our Anglia had a little red badge near the back window, with little silver stars on it.

Jeanette takes a drive down memory lane in a Ford Anglia.

Jackie: I also loved the Ford Zephyr. It had 'shark-like' back tail fins. Aunty Nellie, who lived in Basingstoke and was always a 'cut above the rest', owned one with red leather seats.

Jeanette: Without doubt though, the Mini was one of the most popular cars of the time. They were really loved but were originally very small. I think there was a world record for 27 people managing to squeeze into one, but in general, they could only accommodate four people.

Jackie: We had a beige family Mini. I think most people of our age have had a love affair with the Mini at one time or another, don't you?

Jeanette: Definitely. In fact my first car was a white Mini with the registration KAB 923K which I bought from a lady in Fontmell for £550. I adored it, but must admit that much like today, I seldom looked under the bonnet. I left all that sort of stuff to my darling dad who checked the water, oil and petrol regularly.

Jackie: Minis were very basic. You pulled on a piece of cord to open the doors and there were strange little triangular side windows that you had to push to open. The main windows were operated by manual winders and the heater was operated by a sliding silver knob.

Jeanette: My cousin Wendy's Mini had a dip switch on the floor. I drove back to the Midlands with her one weekend, and it was my job to dip the lights.

Jackie: Seat belts weren't compulsory back then either. In fact, they weren't introduced until the early 70s and even then, wearing them wasn't enforced. There were certainly no rear seat belts. Children and carrycots were simply placed on the back seat.

Jeanette: Most cars had lighters and ashtrays because everyone smoked as they drove along. You also had a choke that needed to be pulled out before turning the ignition key.

Jackie: And then it needed to be pushed back in at the correct time to avoid flooding the engine. I must admit, I never really understood what the choke was all about.

Jeanette: I started driving lessons back in 1973 in a Renault 5, with an instructor from Blandford called Mr Hurley. There was no theory test in those days, but the four main challenges of the actual driving test were the emergency stop, the three-point turn, reversing around a corner, none of which have ever proved useful in my life, and a hill start.

I took my test in Dorchester and passed second time. The first time I got a bit muddled with lanes approaching the roundabout. And you know, I've never liked roundabouts ever since then.

Jackie: I took mine in Salisbury. I passed second time too. The first time, I didn't overtake a tractor on the dual carriageway.

My mum passed her test on her fifth attempt. Until then, she rode a maroon-coloured 'Tina' scooter and wore a white, peaked crash helmet.

Jeanette: I think my mum bought that scooter from her, but she fell off on her first trip and refused to get back on.

Jackie: Well, maybe not everyone's destined to be 'on the road'.

Jeanette: These were the days before satnav, and everyone had an Ordnance Survey road map to find their way around. You planned your route before setting out.

Jackie: You certainly did. And I still love a proper map.

Jeanette: And of course, there were no computerised vehicles. Car mechanics wore overalls covered in oil and grease. In Fontmell, we had The Crown Garage, and it was perfectly normal to see the mechanics smoking on the job.

Jackie: There was always a petrol pump attendant at the garage. No self-service.

Jeanette: And people decorated the car with stickers, or the famous dangly dice in the windscreen or maybe a nodding dog in the back window.

Jackie: As well as the family car we used buses and coaches much more back then. The Sunday school coach outing to Weymouth was a big event. Spotting the first glimpse of a misty blue sea as we came over the crest of the hill outside Weymouth was so exciting.

Jeanette: Although a trip to Weymouth seems pretty run of the mill these days, it was something very special when we were young. At the end of the day, we went to the funfair and there was a ride there called 'The Wild Mouse' which was a really scary type of big dipper. On the way home on the coach, we had a singalong and there would be a 'whip round' for the coach driver's tip.

Jackie: If we went on a day out with the family, we took all our own food and drink. Sandwiches, crisps, cake and biscuits, orange or lemon squash with a Thermos flask of tea for the grown-ups.

Jeanette: Yes, my mum made a mean egg sandwich and we always got sand in them. The only thing we probably bought was an ice cream.

Jackie: We swam in the sea, hired a wooden boat, watched Punch and Judy, built sandcastles and went on the donkey rides. If we were lucky Mum bought us a little packet of paper flags for our sandcastle, a plastic windmill or a stick of rock to take home. I wish I'd kept my first little tin beach bucket which had colourful vintage style images.

Jeanette: It would probably be very rusty by now Jackie.

Did you wear one of those ruched swimsuits which got quite heavy and waterlogged when wet? And those jelly shoes that you had to buckle up?

Jackie: I loved those shoes. But I don't believe Mum or Dad ever wore shorts to the beach. In fact, Dad wore a suit and tie on the beach in the early 60s. Mind you, it was probably just as well because I don't think anyone ever used sun cream or stayed in the shade.

A suit and tie was appropriate beachwear for Jackie's dad on a day trip to Weymouth in 1960.

Jeanette: Everyone wore rubber swimming hats which, for some reason, were bought from the chemist. I can still smell that rubber and have visions of struggling to get my hair covered. And the hat was always fastened with a strap under the chin.

Jackie: Those hats came in several colours, my most memorable was a blue one covered in white rubber flowers. Changing in and out of our swimming costumes meant struggling inside a huge towel with a drawstring top to preserve our modesty.

Jeanette: I hated changing on the beach. When you're young, you always think everyone's watching.

Jackie in her ruched swimsuit.

99

Jeanette with her mum and aunty at the seaside.

Jackie: There was always a lost children hut on the beach and on one trip, our cousin Tony, just a toddler, found himself in the care of the lost children officer. He couldn't tell them his name or anything about himself except that his daddy was a bus driver.

Jeanette: Where else did you go on day trips? I loved Poole Park, especially going for a ride on the little train and also Dad taking us out in a rowing boat. No lifejackets, we lived life dangerously!

Jackie: We often went to Studland and the Bournemouth gardens were my absolute favourite. I thought the little stream and the light displays were magical.

Jeanette: Dad loved to sit in a deckchair and listen to the band playing on the bandstand in Bournemouth gardens.

Jackie: Days trips to the coast were few and far between though. Most Sunday outings involved visiting aunts and uncles for tea, going with Dad on fishing trips to Hanford and Shillingstone or just out in the car 'for a drive'.

Jeanette: What about summer holidays? We went to Blackpool and Plymouth. In fact, we stopped and slept overnight in the car on the way to Blackpool. There was no question of staying in a hotel.

Jackie: That would have cost too much money.

Jeanette: Mum spent most of the holiday shopping for gifts to take home and she loved browsing all the saucy seaside postcards.

Jackie: I longed to go to a Butlin's holiday camp after seeing a brochure and being seduced by the blue of the swimming pools. We didn't venture abroad, well only as far as Jersey. We went to Cornwall a couple of times where we stayed in a holiday camp. I loved being able to go to the clubhouse on the site as it meant we could stay up late. We often stayed with Aunty Dolly who ran a bed and breakfast in South Shields.

Jeanette: It's a shame we have so few photographs of those days. I guess because cameras, and film, were quite expensive. You could go through the long process of getting them developed at the chemist and then find half of them were rubbish.

Jackie: Well, it seems that the staycation is now quite popular again.

Jeanette: A whole new generation is appreciating the same British seaside that we enjoyed growing up. And the beauty is…most places are within driving distance.

Jackie's sister Sue, on an outing, posing with a monkey.

11

A Family Affair

'Brides were often given a silver horseshoe on a ribbon, a little chimney sweep or black cat for luck...'

Imagine a wedding where...
The bride leaves for the honeymoon wearing a special 'going away' outfit.
The bride and groom leave the reception before it ends.
The reception is a simple buffet in the local village hall.
The local newspaper lists each and every guest.

Jackie: You went to my sister's wedding at Compton didn't you?

Jeanette: Yes I did. She wore a big floppy hat. And didn't your mum make all the dresses?

Flowers and floppy hats: bridesmaid Jackie, left, at sister Sue's wedding at Compton Church in 1972.

Jackie: Yes, and she also made the groom's brown velvet suit. I was a bridesmaid and wore a dark yellow seersucker dress with artificial flowers in my hair and in a hand basket, very trendy at the time.

Jeanette: That was 1972 and of course weddings were much more low key, more home-made. The dresses, the catering, a lot less money was spent than today.

Jackie: My sister had her reception at the Royal Chase Hotel in Shaftesbury. She had lots of sparkling wine from Spain because she was working at Bath Travel in Bournemouth at the time and so had it brought over.

Jeanette: Sparkling wine would have been very posh.

Jackie: We often went to Highbridge in Somerset to the wedding of one of Aunty Kathy's 10 children. We all piled into the back of a van. I'd probably be wearing a homemade dress and white sandals. Aunties were probably wearing crimplene suits and always a hat. The men wore a suit; three-piece suits with a waistcoat were very popular in the 70s.

Jeanette: Cousin Barbara held her reception in Compton Village Hall, I think she borrowed Aunty Jean's wedding dress. The dress was quite unusual as it was just below the knee and full skirted, late 50s style.

Jackie: Of course, you and I were fellow bridesmaids at cousin Diane's wedding at Compton. I think it was 1969. I wore a turquoise dress made of some sort of man-made fabric with matching shoes.

Jeanette: I wore lemon and we both had our hair in ringlets held with a comb of fabric flowers. Cousin Jane was the little bridesmaid and wore pink, and the matron of honour wore blue. It was all very colourful.

Jackie: The bride and groom followed the tradition at St Mary's Church and planted a tree in the church grounds. My mum and dad, who married in the 50s, and Aunty Nellie and Uncle Ken, planted cherry trees either side of the church gate when they married there. The trees produced beautiful blooms for many years until they succumbed to disease and had to be removed. My sister's tree and cousin Diane's still remain.

Jeanette and Jackie left, fellow bridesmaids for cousin Diane at Compton Church in 1969.

Jeanette: We threw confetti which came in a little box by Deeko with tiny paper horseshoes and wedding bells.

Jackie: Brides were often given a silver horseshoe on a ribbon, a little chimney sweep or black cat for luck, which they held with their bouquet.

Jeanette: I don't think the groom had a wedding ring, whether that was because of cost or fashion, I'm not sure.

Jackie: Stag and hen 'dos' weren't very common. The groom might have gone down the pub the night before, but there certainly weren't expensive, multiple foreign trips for the wedding party like there are today.

Jeanette: Another lost tradition is the 'bottom drawer'. Girls used to collect household goods ready for married life.

Jackie: Oh my goodness, I'd forgotten the 'bottom drawer'. These days couples have everything they need by the time they marry.

Jeanette: Back then wedding presents were very important as most couples weren't already living together and needed everything to set up house. Wedding lists were kept at various shops, and guests often just bought maybe one plate as part of a dinner service. Nobody would dream of giving cash as a gift.

Jackie: The bride also had a trousseau which included underwear and some outfits for the honeymoon.

Jeanette: There certainly weren't such things as 'save the date' cards, just invitations that needed to be formally acknowledged and of course children were always invited.

Family wedding reception at Fontmell Village Hall.

Jackie: Village halls were usually the venue for receptions and if it was a buffet there were probably vol-au-vents, sandwiches, sausage rolls and a three-tier white-iced wedding cake with a plastic bride and groom standing on the top. If you were invited and couldn't make the wedding, a piece of wedding cake in a little box would be posted to you.

Jeanette: Often the family prepared the food.

Jackie: The 'top table' today is often much more complicated. Back then, everyone simply sat in one long line. Nowadays, there are all sorts of different arrangements.

Bridesmaid Jeanette, 70s style.

Jeanette: It was tradition for the best man to read out telegrams from people who couldn't attend. These were usually short and sweet as the post office charged by the word.

Jackie: Everyone drank too much and drove home, nobody thought anything of it. I don't think there were ever taxis waiting to take guests home.

Jeanette: The couple left before the end of the reception, the bride in a smart suit with hat and gloves, and the couple's car might be decorated with tin cans and have 'just married' scrawled over it.

Jackie: And if they were staying nearby, family might have 'messed up' the marital bed, which seems really quite silly.

Granny Hardiman with sisters Florrie and Edie. Crimplene suits and little hats were usual for wedding guests in the 60s and 70s.

Jeanette: Wedding photography was very formal, family groups rather than reportage style. Of course, we were lucky enough to have cousin Heather whose hobby was cine film and who recorded several family weddings. But in general, the couple waited weeks for their photos and then they'd be put in an album with each photo protected by a sheet of tissue paper.

Jackie: The whole wedding was reported by the local paper, the *Western Gazette,* from the guest list to what the bride wore, whether the dress was Empire line, Dupont, A-line, short veil etc. right through to what the couple did for a living and where they were going on honeymoon.

Jeanette: Well at least we've now managed to track down cousin Heather's cine films of all the family weddings.

Jackie: What a trip down memory lane that's going to be.

12

Say Cheese!

*'People even held slide shows so friends and neighbours could find out what
happened on foreign holidays..'*

Imagine photography when…
*Cine, slides and cameras are the only means of capturing events on film.
You wait a week while your films are being developed at the chemist.
There's only one photographer's studio in town.
Only black and white photos are available.*

Jackie: I always say that if my house was on fire, the first thing I'd grab, after family and pets, would be my photo albums. There's nothing more precious or irreplaceable. I most probably feel that way because we have so few photos from our childhood.

Jeanette: There's something special about a photograph, capturing a moment in time.

Jackie: Pre-digital, photography was quite a 'hit and miss' affair, wasn't it? Cameras and film were relatively expensive and there was no guarantee, after you'd had your film developed at the chemist, that you'd get decent results.

Jeanette: Mr Bealing was the only photographer around during my childhood. He had a studio in Salisbury Street, Shaftesbury and that was where we were taken for formal shots.

Jackie: I've got a black and white photo taken by him, I must have been about six years old, hair in long plaits with ribbons, best shift dress on and holding a little toy monkey, there was always a prop to hold or, for babies, a couch to lie on with flowing gown and matinee jacket perfectly positioned.

Jeanette: What about school photos? I don't think anyone made sure we were prepared to be photographed, mine were terrible.

Jeanette and brother David. Everyone went to Bealing's in Salisbury Street for family photoshoots.

Jackie: When my own children had school photos taken, I'd send them off with a comb and strict instructions to look presentable before their photo was taken. I don't think my parents were warned about the school photographer's visits as my first black and white photo from Fontmell School shows a little girl with cropped hair, sticking up in tufts.

Jeanette: At Shaftesbury High School we were lined up on the netball courts in a huge semi-circle with teachers arranged at the front. It's always good fun to unroll the long school photo and try to identify everyone.

Jackie: I think the earliest photo of me is when I was a few months old, sitting in my pram in the front garden at Capstitch in Compton.

Jeanette: Slides were another popular format in the 60s and 70s. People even held slide shows so friends and neighbours could find out what happened on foreign holidays, particularly if the trip had been to somewhere exotic like Australia. In Fontmell there was a couple, Mr and Mrs Goodrich, who held a film show after they'd been on holiday to New Zealand. I think most of the villagers attended.

Jackie: We led sheltered lives.

Jeanette and Jackie's primary school photos.

Jeanette: My first camera was a little Box Brownie. Cameras were always worn on a strap around your neck and the really expensive ones had a leather case.

Jackie: Films were bought from the chemist and came in 12, 24 and 36 exposures. I was always told the film should be changed in a dark room to ensure it wasn't exposed to the light. You opened the back and threaded the film on to the spool and after every photo you needed to wind the film on. No wonder we often ended up with one photo superimposed on top of another.

Jeanette: And flash bulbs had to be attached to the camera separately. They were usually bought in a box of three. And then a new type of camera came on the market which included a flash. It was rectangular with a carrying strap. I think it was called a Kodak Instamatic.

Jackie: I thought Polaroid cameras were just magic. You could watch the photo develop in front of your eyes. Well, that was after you'd waved it about to dry!

Jeanette: Photos from the 70s all seemed to have an orange tinge, whether that was the camera or the fact that we put them in those awful photo albums under sticky plastic film. The old albums had a sheet of tissue paper to protect the photos and little photo corners to keep your pictures in place.

Slides were popular in the 70s. Often, people returning from exotic holidays hosted slideshows for fellow villagers.

Jackie: Photo booths were another bit of magic where you could collect your strip of photos after just a few minutes. There can't be many of our baby boomer generation who don't have a few of those pictures where we crammed inside, larked about and pulled a face.

Jeanette: The video camera came on the scene in the 70s. It was still quite a large piece of equipment and, of course, by the end of the 70s, you could watch your video on your very own video player.

Jackie: Now that really was 'state of the art' stuff!

Jackie and toy 'prop' at Bealing's photographers in Salisbury Street, Shaftesbury.

Jeanette with the familiar panelled backdrop at Bealing's photographers in Salisbury Street, Shaftesbury.

13

The Folks Who Lived on The Hill

'My aunty maintains that asking for a packet of Polos was code for 'something for the weekend' but I'm not sure how true that is.'

Imagine Gold Hill and St James, Shaftesbury...
When there are two grocery shops in the street.
When all the houses are family homes.
When everyone knows everyone else.
In a time before the Hovis advert.

Jackie: I suppose Shaftesbury was rather like your second home when you were growing up.

Jeanette: Yes, especially Gold Hill and St James. In fact, St James's Church is quite a special place for me. I was christened there

Gold Hill, Shaftesbury in the early 60s.

and not only are my parents' ashes buried there, my grandfather's grave is there and both my parents and my maternal grandparents were married there.

Christening day for Jeanette with Aunty Joan at St James's Church.

Jackie: Your maternal grandparents lived on Gold Hill didn't they?

Jeanette: Yes, Nan and Grandad lived at 17A Gold Hill, and I have nothing but fond memories of that house. On Saturdays, people called in to visit Nan from dawn till dusk. Everyone just rang the bell and walked in. The baker, the butcher, deliveries from the shop, friends and family; everyone was welcome. My nan was well-loved and never stood on ceremony. She enjoyed the company of others so much.

Jackie: But they also lived at the bottom of the hill at one time didn't they?

Jeanette: Yes, at one time, they owned Gold Hill Cottage, just across the road at the foot of the hill. My parents lived in the annexe of that cottage for the first few years of their marriage with my brother. It had a massive, cottage garden to the rear with a separate barn or garage that's now been converted to a holiday home.

Jackie: I bet Gold Hill was completely different in the 60s and 70s.

Jeanette: My grandparents knew most of the neighbours who lived on the hill. Today, it's full of holiday lets but, in those days, it was a real community with people popping in and out of each other's houses. Family names that spring to mind are Davidson, Kimber, Gumbleton, Thorne and Hallett.

Jackie: And of course, I suppose your grandparents' house was quite basic, unlike today when properties on Gold Hill are extremely desirable.

Jeanette: That's right. There weren't many mod cons in 17A. No running hot water and just one toilet, adjoining the kitchen. At night, you'd take a bucket or chamber pot up to bed with you just in case you got 'caught short' and couldn't make it down the stairs. That was just the way it was.

The view of St James's area from Park Walk

Jackie: Was there a big garden?

Jeanette: There was a small, gravelled yard with a coal bunker in the corner. We often sat out there in deck chairs when it was sunny and it's so amusing to think that when the house went up for sale years later, the humble yard was described as a 'walled garden'. Nan would have chuckled at that. But 17A and the house next door are still the only two houses on the hill with parking, which is quite an asset.

Jackie: Were you around when the Hovis advert was filmed?

Jeanette: It seems strange, but that filming passed me by. I think, like most locals at the time, I was so used to seeing people filming on the hill, it meant nothing to me. But I know that all the aerials were removed from the houses before filming started and of course, many people to this day, believe the advert was filmed 'up north'.

Jackie: Did you see any other filming?

Jeanette: When they filmed *Far From the Madding Crowd* in 1967, I stood outside 17A and watched Terence Stamp come down the hill on horseback with his unit. And our younger cousin, Jane, a baby at the time, was an extra, being taken up the hill in a handcart.

Jackie: Yes, my older sister Sue took time out from the secondary modern school to watch the filming. You were probably able to stay with your grandparents to watch all the goings-on.

Jeanette: I stayed there most Fridays. Most Saturday mornings my nan sent me down the street to the shop with her weekly grocery order. The shop was next to the post box that's still there and was run by Mr and Mrs Brown. I can picture them immediately. She had blue/grey hair, wore a white overall and bright red lipstick. He had little round spectacles. She had quite a reputation as a bit of a rogue because no matter what she weighed out, whether fruit, vegetables or sweets, it was frequently 'just over' and she would charge for it of course. Our aunty Jean's convinced that's how she made her money.

Family line-up in the yard at 17A Gold Hill with Jeanette 2nd from left.

Jackie: And were there other shops in the street?

Jeanette: Further up the road, there was another shop run by Mr and Mrs Gray, but for some reason, I didn't go in there very often, probably because my nan didn't buy from them either. They sold exactly the same items as the Browns, so I guess it was a little friendly, harmless competition in the street.

Jackie: Wasn't there a barber in St James too?

Jeanette: Yes, on the corner of White Hart Lane, there was a tiny wooden hut which was a barber shop and that was run by a man called Bert Mayo. He was a very short gentleman, with greased-back, black hair.

Besides cutting hair, he sold sweets and I think maybe cigarettes. Aunty Jean maintains that asking for a packet of Polos was code for 'something for the weekend' but I'm not sure how true that is.

Jackie: And much like Gold Hill, I suppose the cottages in the street were family homes at that time.

Jeanette: Yes they were, with names like Jolliffe, Dooley and Alford living there. Of course, although The Pump Yard is now a landmark, back then those cottages were family homes too, often with outside toilets.

Golden Wedding celebrations, 17A Gold Hill, in The Western Gazette.

Jackie: How times have changed.

Jeanette: If my grandparents could return now and take a look at Gold Hill, they'd be amazed at the property prices. Although the hill itself has changed very little, it's no longer a neighbourhood, but much more of a tourist attraction.

Jackie: That's progress.

Jeanette and Nan Sims in the back yard at 17A Gold Hill.

Beautiful Gold Hill.

14
High Street Stroll

'It was quite normal for people to stand outside the shop and watch the TV. You could amuse yourself for hours.'

Imagine Shaftesbury High Street when...
Greengrocers display their goods on a ledge outside the shop.
Shops are closed at lunchtimes and on Wednesday afternoons.
King Alfred's Kitchen is the main coffee shop.
There's one small supermarket.

Jackie: How did the High Street look in the 60s and 70s?

Jeanette: There were definitely fewer tea and coffee shops. King Alfred's Kitchen was there and Anstee's, in Angel Square down the bottom of the High Street had a little café area. As teenagers we congregated there for hours buying just one cup of coffee

ANSTEES BAKERS
ANGEL SQUARE
SHAFTESBURY

Quality Own Baked Bread & Cakes
and Savoury Goods
Wedding & Birthday Cakes

Tea & Coffee Bar at Rear of Shop

Jackie: Anstee's used to bake their bread in Angel Lane. I can picture George in the bakery in his white trilby and overalls. And I can still see those huge silver metal mixers and machines through the doorway in Angel Lane.

The bakery's long gone and several cottages now stand on that site. In fact, they've been named in honour of the bakery. But that amazing smell wafting out of the building is totally unforgettable and brings back so many memories.

Jeanette: Their shop premises were actually two separate units. The main part was the bakers, selling wonderful bread and cakes. But at the side, facing on to Salisbury Street, was a tiny sweet shop called Smales which was very popular with high school and grammar school pupils walking between buildings.

Jackie: And further along the road at 28 Salisbury Street there was a hairdressing salon called Barbara's.

Jeanette: I think at some point, that salon was also called Condell Hair Fashions.

Jackie: There was also Richard Miles' hair salon, in The Commons, above the chemist. It was very 'pink'.

Jeanette: I'm not sure that I ever visited Richard Miles. It seemed very exclusive and only certain ladies went there.

Shaftesbury Town Hall with its low wall and public conveniences on either side.

Jackie: I think there was another hairdressing salon called Marjorie and Nora, further down the High Street at number 52.

Jeanette: Opposite Barbara's in Salisbury Street, was Gus Bealing's Photography Studio where most locals went.

Jackie: Well we were certainly well off for sweet shops. Peach's was located just across the road from Anstee's at 63 High Street and also included what is now the adjoining property. And further up the town in The Commons, there was Joyce Phillips which was extremely popular with school children.

Jeanette: Later on, that shop moved around the corner to smaller premises at 2 The Commons, in Bell Street. There was also a shop called Hailstones at 11 High Street, which sold sweets, papers, books and a few toys.

Jackie: Many sweets weren't pre-packed. They'd be stored in big glass jars standing on shelves around the shop and the shopkeeper used a metal scoop to dig them out. Things like pineapple chunks, mint imperials, aniseed balls, rhubarb and custard, sherbet lemons, pear drops, barley sugar, clove balls and loads of other favourites of the time.

Jeanette: You'd usually ask for a quarter (quarter of a pound), and they'd be weighed out on the scales and poured into a little white bag.

Jackie: But these were also the days of the 'penny tray' and you could enjoy four Black Jacks, or Fruit Cocktail chews for one old penny.

Jeanette: Or if you had threepence, you could get a Milky Way or some fruit Polos.

Jackie: An 'after-school' treat was often some fruit gums or pastilles. Or maybe Spangles or Opal Fruits. And horrific though it seems now, sweet cigarettes were very popular and came with a collectable card.

Jeanette: I loved those Jamboree Bags that contained an assortment of sweets and came with a free toy. Also Bazooka Joe bubble gum or Beech Nut chewing gum.

Jackie: My favourite chocolate bars were Caramac and Cadbury's Fruit and Nut, all of which were much chunkier than they are today.

Jeanette: Grandad always ate sugared almonds, which were really hard, or butterscotch, which I thought were only for old people. I'm sure he bought them because he knew we children wouldn't eat them.

Jackie: My dad always had a crumpled paper bag of extra strong mints in his pocket.

Jeanette: Ah, what sweet memories.

Jackie: What about fruit and veg shops? Everyone shopped in town for their greens, there was absolutely no question of popping to the supermarket.

Jeanette: Brickell's greengrocers was down the bottom end of town at 56A High Street. I think they were next door to Hussey's pet shop which stood on the corner of Angel Square at 58 High Street.

Jackie: They also sold coal which was stored in the yard behind the shop.

Jeanette: Further on up the town were some other greengrocers. W. Welch, at 4 Church Lane and Robinson's, almost opposite at 12 High

Street and around the corner, opposite Bell Street car park, was Abbott's.

Jackie: The ledges outside the shops were overflowing with lovely fruit and veg.

Jeanette: And opposite Hussey's at 63 High Street, at one time there were two shops. On one side was a ladies' boutique and on the other side was Multi-Electrics.

Jackie: What about Granada TV? That was just up the street at 54B High Street. We used to rent a TV from there.

Jeanette: Everyone used to rent a TV because they were considered a luxury item. And later on in the 70s you could rent a video recorder too.

Jackie: It was quite normal for people to stand outside the shop and watch the TV. You could amuse yourself for hours.

Jeanette: And good old Cordery's was opposite at 51 High Street. A truly traditional drapers and outfitters and so quirky with those uneven floors all over the place.

Jackie: They stocked cottons, wools, fabrics, buttons, ribbons and other haberdashery, everything you could possibly need, all displayed in marvellous wooden, glass-topped cabinets and loads of drawers.

Jeanette: Opposite Cordery's, just a little further up the street at number 50 was Kelley's bakers who made and sold the most scrumptious currant buns. I'm sure they produced many other delicious cakes and bread, but to me, those currant buns outshone everything else. I've never tasted currant buns like them since.

Jackie: Now WHSmith hasn't ever moved, has it? They've always been just a bit further up the town at 42 High Street.

Jeanette: That's right. But in the 60s and 70s, there was a little kiosk at the side of the shop selling magazines and newspapers. I think a metal shutter was pulled down at closing time.

Jackie: I always loved the smell of the new books in Smiths. Didn't your aunty Gladys work there?

Jeanette: Yes, Aunty Gladys worked there for years.

Jackie: Wasn't there a butcher's shop opposite Smiths?

Jeanette: Baxter's I think. The lady cashier sat in a little kiosk, with a glass window, separate from the rest of the shop.

Jackie: Oh, so the butchers didn't have to touch the money.

Jeanette: That's right. And I'm sure there was sawdust on the floor you know. Of course, there was another butcher's shop called Eastman's at 3 High Street, the top of Tout Hill.

Jeanette: Nan bought 'lights' which are offal, from the butcher to feed the cat. She never bought tinned food.

Jackie: My mum did the same or got fish scraps to boil up for the cats. The only cat food Mum bought was Katkins because there were no dried food or 'gourmet' brands.

Jeanette: Further up the town, nearer to the town hall, at 29-31 there was Squire's, the men's outfitters, which of course is still there as we speak.

Jackie: That's so iconic. Bit like good old Hine and Parsons which used to be across the road at 28 and 30 High Street.

The iconic Hine & Parsons paper bag.

Jeanette: I suppose it was probably the closest to a department store that Shaftesbury's ever had. I think that at one time, before Shirley Allum took over part of the building, they also sold women's clothes.

Jackie: Just a bit further down from Hine and Parsons at 32 High Street was John Jeffery's marvellous salesroom. I often visited with Gran Hardiman to take a look at the lots. I loved shuffling through things like vinyl records, old books and crockery.

Jeanette: I still have a wardrobe that my maternal grandmother bought second-hand in there, so goodness knows how old it is now.

Jackie: Just along the pavement at 26A High Street was Allum's, which later changed to Allum and Sidaway. That's been there for years.

Jeanette: When I passed my 11+ exam, Mum and Dad told me I could go to Allum's and buy a piece of jewellery as a reward. I spent £3.50 (then it was £3 10s) on a gold signet ring which I still have.

Jackie: What about Frisby's shoe shop? It was right next door to Allum's at number 26. I spent hours staring through the window because it was right by the bus stop.

Jeanette: It was run by Mr and Mrs Arthur.

Jackie: It was the place your mum took you to have your feet measured on one of those little sloping footstools with the sliding ruler. Then you'd probably choose a pair of Clarks shoes.

Frisby's shoe shop and Bridle's toy shop, Shaftesbury.

Jeanette: Do you know, I still have a metal shoehorn with the name 'Frisby's' engraved on it, probably now an antique?

Jackie: There was also Bagshaw's further down the town, but I don't think they were particularly popular with the younger generation.

Jeanette: Let's face it, neither Frisby's or Bagshaw's were really very trendy.

Jackie: No, Shaftesbury's never had a great range of shoe shops.

Jeanette: In the late 60s, next door to Frisby's at 22–24 High Street, there was a toy shop called Bridle's.

Jackie: I thought that was a furniture shop called Stratton's.

Jeanette: I think that was later when it opened as Stratton Sons & Mead and stretched round the corner to the premises at 16A High Street.

Jackie: And there were two chemist shops in town. Boots was situated at 14 High Street and round the corner at 6 The Commons there was Hitchin's which had Richard Miles, the hairdressing salon above.

Jeanette: Just opposite at 6 Bell Street there was The Colour Centre which sold paint, wallpaper and other DIY materials.

Jackie: Of course, shops like B&Q and Homebase didn't exist, so this was the best place to go if you were intending to do some home decoration.

Jeanette: There was a distinct shortage of ladies' clothes shops in the town, but opposite The Colour Centre in Bell Street there was Chesterfield White which sold a limited selection of fashions for the more mature lady and lots of baby and children's clothes. Often, I was sent there to collect a garment for my grandmother and she'd often have the item 'on appro' which was jargon for 'on approval'. 'Chesterfield White' is still painted on the wall above where the shop used to be.

Jackie: But the shops always had half day closing on a Wednesday and would probably be closed between 1 and 2 for lunch.

Jeanette: Can't imagine that going down very well today. People nowadays demand shops to be open all hours.

Jackie: We're lucky really, here in Shaftesbury, there's always been a lovely mixture of shops in the High Street.

Jeanette: And long may it continue.

15
Wear Your Tassel with Pride

'If you went out with one of the Grammar School boys, you swapped scarf tassels. So, you could tell by the number of blue tassels on your scarf, how many boys you'd been out with.'

Imagine a school where...
Weeding the garden is one of the punishments for bad behaviour.
Badges are awarded to pupils who are well-groomed.
Many lessons are held in Portakabins®.
Sixth formers rule with 'a rod of iron'.

Shaftesbury High School, as it was when Jeanette and Jackie were pupils.

Jeanette: Miss Woods, the headmistress at Shaftesbury High School, had her office to the left of the front door in the main house, which still stands in the Bell Street car park. And the staff room was the other side of the door. I can still smell the coffee and cigarette smoke. Those smells wafted out whenever the staff room door was opened.

Jackie: You only visited those rooms if you'd been given a detention, which meant that you had to weed the flower borders or something similar.

Jeanette: I think I ended up sitting outside the headmistress's office on more than one occasion. She lived above her office in a flat, didn't she?

Jackie: Yes, but we were never allowed up there.

Jeanette: I think the original front door is still there. There used to be a brass ship's bell hanging by the door which one of the sixth form girls had to ring at the end of each lesson. I wonder what's happened to that bell?

Jackie: I hope someone's kept it. It should be a treasured museum piece.

Jeanette: We used to laugh if they forgot to ring it, or if they rang it in a strange way. Young girls laugh at such silly things, don't they?

Jeanette: It was a wonderful garden. And there was a beautiful weeping willow tree hanging over the lawn in front of the house.

COMEDY IN DELIGHTFUL SETTING

The pupils of Shaftesbury High School for Girls act out a scene from Sheridan's ...tty comedy, 'The Critic', in the delightful setting of the school gardens. The play, 'oduced by Mrs. R. Wild, was presented in the School Hall on Wednesday and 'sterday (Thursday) and will be ....

Shaftesbury High School girls perform under the willow tree in the school grounds.

An exhibition at Shaftesbury Town Museum, showing a Shaftesbury High School uniform. Both the hat and scarf have tassels.

Jackie: There was also a side gate with access to Parsons Pool. And a couple of extra classrooms in the gardens. Then there was a path leading from those classrooms, winding through the gardens, past the senior library, the netball court and down some steps in front of the domestic science room.

Jeanette: We used the Parsons Pool entrance if we were walking up to Barton Hill where I think there were another two classrooms, well, temporary Portakabins® really. I seem to recall the art room was one of them.

Jackie: That senior library was really just an outhouse in the garden with a sort of glass conservatory on the front and the domestic science room was also a Portakabin®. At the side of the Domestic Science room there was the main school entrance, now part of the car park wall. We used that entrance at the start and end of day and also at lunchtimes when we were marched, crocodile-style, across the road to the canteen behind the house which at that time was the senior boarding house.

Jeanette: In the canteen, there was a sixth-former on each table to make sure we behaved ourselves.

Jackie: I loved school dinners. In fact, I'd often finish up friends' plates, especially when it was beef stew which, looking back, was mainly gristle.

Jeanette: Later on, Oslo lunches were introduced, and I started having those instead.

Jackie: Wasn't that soup, cheese, salad, bread and an apple? I suppose it seemed a lower calorie option.

Jeanette: Probably. Those sixth-formers were like the police though.

Jackie: Even on the school bus we had to wear our hats or they reported us. Those hats were like skull caps with a red tassel. They were awful. In fact, they now have one on show in Gold Hill Museum.

Jeanette: Ah, the school bus, I got on at Fontmell and you jumped on at Compton.

Jackie: I was absolutely terrified on my first day at Shaftesbury High. I got on the bus, which was packed, and you tapped the person next to you on the shoulder and said 'budge over and let her sit down'.

Jeanette: That was so nice of me.

Jackie: Yes, it was a lovely thing to do. But I don't think you ever saved me a seat again.

Shaftesbury Grammar School for Boys.

Jeanette: You always bought the school blazer about five sizes too big. Mum said I'd grow into it, and she was right actually, I think it lasted me about six years.

Jackie's blazer - getting shorter in the arms by the time she was in the fifth form at Shaftesbury High School.

Jackie: Our parents had to buy lots of sports' equipment as well.

Jeanette: Track suit, hockey stick, hockey boots, aertex blouses, blue wrap-around PE skirts. The list was endless really. I think I still have my scarf somewhere.

Jackie: I think I do too. And of course, if you went out with one of the grammar school boys, who had blue scarves, you'd swap tassels. So, you could tell by the number of blue tassels on your scarf, how many boys you'd been out with.

Jeanette: Well, I could certainly tell … because I didn't have any.

Jackie: Neither did I.

Jeanette: But you know what, Jackie, considering this school was supposedly the 'crème de la crème' and you'd made it if you'd passed your 11+, it had no on-site facilities. We spent our days walking along Barton Hill, to and from lessons. And we'd trail all the way up Wincombe Lane to the hockey field and break the ice before starting to play.

Jackie: I think that field was opposite Ten Acres, where there's now a housing estate. It was huge and open to the elements and so windy and cold. In fact, the coldest place in Shaftesbury I reckon.

Jeanette: And we certainly didn't have much protection from that hockey ball.

Jackie: No helmets or anything like that. Only the goalie had shin pads.

Jeanette: I did enjoy netball though. I played Goal Attack. What position were you?

Jackie: I was Goal Defence. We used to wear those tabards with the initials of our position on them.

Jeanette: Goodness yes. We had to tie the bows at each side.

Jackie: Yes, and the netball court was where the long-stay Bell Street car park is now located. It doubled up as a tennis court, didn't it?

Jeanette: Yes, although we also used to play tennis up at Barton Hill recreation ground. There were a few courts up there.

Jackie: I hated gym more than anything.

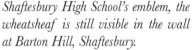
Shaftesbury High School's emblem, the wheatsheaf is still visible in the wall at Barton Hill, Shaftesbury.

Jeanette: Me too. In fact, the PE teacher gave up on my form and let us do country dancing instead. We used the Stalbridge Hut, which is now the Shaston Social Club. All that gym equipment just terrified me.

Jackie: There was the box, the parallel bars, the climbing bars, the ropes. Oh, and the horse, which for some reason was stored in one of the cloakrooms.

Jeanette: We just walked around it, as if it wasn't there. Big brown suede thing.

Jackie: Amazingly, there were absolutely no shower facilities at that school.

Jeanette: It must have been awful to have a PE lesson and then have to get back into our uniform.

Jackie: But we never questioned it.

Jeanette: We had three school houses didn't we? Wren, Hardy and Barnes. I was in Hardy, which was green.

Jackie: I was in Hardy too. Wren was blue and Barnes was yellow.

Catching some sun outside the senior library at Shaftesbury High School.

Jeanette: And we wore some kind of sash around the waist to show which house we belonged to.

Jackie: For some reason, those sashes were called girdles.

Jeanette: Of course, we studied specific books for our exams. I think we read *Lord of the Flies* for 'O' level. And I loved *Pride and Prejudice* and anything by Dickens.

Jackie: I loved reading *My Family and Other Animals* and also *The Crucible*. But I also enjoyed Shakespeare and Chaucer.

Jeanette: I won the annual reading competition twice. I think I read from *What Katy Did*.

Jackie: You're such a talent, Jeanette.

Jeanette: The other thing we didn't have was a swimming pool. We went to the town baths for lessons and for our swimming gala. I think I was competing in the back crawl one year and ended up tangled in the ropes. Very embarrassing.

Jackie: Miss Fraser, who taught us maths and who was quite a large lady, dived in to save somebody one year. I've never forgotten that she took the time to remove her watch first.

Jeanette: Did we ever have a sports day at Shaftesbury High?

Shaftesbury High School pupils who cruised on SS Uganda in the early 70s.

Jackie: I think so. Maybe up at Wincombe Lane. There was the shot put and also the javelin. In fact, I think somebody got hit by a javelin one year.

Jeanette: I missed that. I think I must have been hiding.

Jackie: Maybe in the horse!

Jeanette: Then of course, we had our carol service at Holy Trinity Church, with the Grammar School. And speech day at the old Savoy Cinema on Bimport. So much walking around to various buildings in Shaftesbury.

Jackie: I mean, it must have been a 10-minute walk from the main school to the Barton Hill classrooms, in all weathers.

Jeanette: We just roamed around the town. Parents today wouldn't allow it. Mind you, we often used to nip into a sweet shop on the way to class.

Barton Hill boarding house in Shaftesbury.

Jackie: And thinking about the main school building, there were really higgledy-piggledy stairs leading to some of the classrooms. In fact, one or two of the classrooms were in the attic space.

Jackie: We always had an end-of-term film. Long before the days of downloading or streaming, the film was shown in the school hall on a big, white, roll down screen, using a projector.

Jeanette: I know we had film favourites like *Flipper*, a popular dolphin of the time and *Romeo and Juliet*, with Leonard Whiting and Olivia Hussey.

Jackie: And there was always a special end of term assembly. We sang the school hymn, 'Jerusalem'.

Jeanette: We also had a speech day, held at the Savoy Cinema, which parents attended and where various prizes were handed out to worthy winners. Do you know, Jackie, I always longed for a deportment star. They were awarded to girls who carried themselves elegantly and were well-groomed. Sadly, I was never a recipient.

Jackie: I never managed to get one of those either.

Shaftesbury County Modern School (later Christy's School).

Jeanette: One other thing that sticks in my mind about end of term, is the mandatory trip around 'confiscation' which was basically all the items that we'd left hanging around the school throughout the term. You had to look at all the 'lost' stuff that was still unclaimed and spot anything that belonged to you.

Jackie: That's it. Throughout the term, any items left in changing rooms or elsewhere were collected and placed in confiscation. Then once a week (I believe it was on a Friday lunchtime) any pupils who had lost items took a look in confiscation and paid to get the item back. I think it cost a penny.

Jeanette: The main hall was used for both gym and morning assembly, which took place every day.

Jackie: And there were the honours boards all around the hall, with the names and qualifications of ex-pupils who had graduated from university.

Jeanette: Oh, Jackie. We never made it on to one of those boards.

Jackie: No, we didn't, but we did ok!

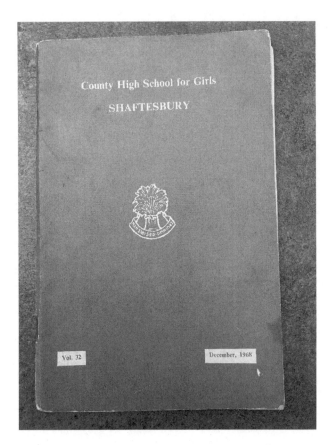

Shaftesbury High School magazine December 1968.

16
Why Do I Need to Know This?

'Who needs a mobile phone when there's semaphore?'

Imagine a time when...
Tacking stitches are a vital part of the sewing process.
You earn a 'hostess' award for making a cup of tea.
Instead of texting you use flags to send messages.
Logarithms are a necessary part of life.

Jackie: Did you learn semaphore at Brownies?

Jeanette: Gosh yes. What was the point of all that?

Jackie: You had little flags on sticks, and you could send messages by positioning them in various ways. Did you ever use it?

Jeanette: No, I didn't. But you know, I guess that if ever you happen to be on Park Walk, Shaftesbury and I'm down in St James, you could give it a whirl and send me a message.

Jackie: Who needs a mobile phone when there's semaphore?

Jeanette: That was just one of the curious skills we learnt at Brownies. There were also all those different knots that we've never used and the art of lighting a fire. We got badges for everything didn't we? And you had to sew them on your uniform sleeve.

Jackie: I only got one badge while I was in the Brownies. That was my 'hostess' badge which involved visiting an elderly lady in Fontmell Magna, making her a cup of tea and serving it to her on a tray.

Jeanette: I didn't stay in the Brownies too long. I got told off for switching the lights on and off.

Jackie: So, you left in disgrace.

Jeanette: No. I left with my head held high and I never went back.

Brownies and Guides at a presentation event in Compton Village Hall.

Jackie: I never made it to the Guides.

Jeanette: Me neither. Maybe we just weren't the right types for all those exciting challenges.

But another skill that we learnt was how to tie a tie.

Jackie: You never forget that do you?

Jeanette: No, although I don't think I undid my tie properly for about five years when I was at Shaftesbury High. I think most of us just loosened them and pulled them over our heads.

Jackie: It's a bit like riding a bike.

Jeanette: Riding a bike. Wasn't there a cycling proficiency test or something that everyone used to try and pass?

Jackie: Yes. I think the test taught you how to ride in and out of bollards, cones and other obstacles.

Jeanette: I know there was something called Knights of the Road and although I didn't take the test, my brother and some friends did it. If they passed, they got a badge in the shape of a knight's head.

Jackie: I suppose there were other skills we learnt as we grew up like tying shoelaces and bows. They're all there in our memory bank, aren't they?

A Guiding event at Fontmell Village Hall.

Mementos from Guides and Brownies.

Jackie's mum, Tawny Owl for Fontmell Brownies, and sister Sue in Guide uniform.

Jeanette: What about stuff we learnt at school though? So many forgotten things like logarithms.

Jackie: Algebra.

Jeanette: Trigonometry.

Jackie: We had special little books to help us. But it was all nonsense to me.

Jeanette: When do we ever use any of it in daily life now? And if we did, would we need one of those special books to help us out?

Jeanette: Well, you know, I always wish I'd studied Latin.

Jackie: Me too. It's a real basic for every language, isn't it? And I'm not sure why we had to learn how to write things in French, it makes much more sense to focus on speaking doesn't it?

Jeanette: I've often thought about that. When I took my French 'O' level oral exam, I was terrified, purely because we'd done loads of writing and hardly any speaking.

But you know what I really wish?

Jackie: What's that?

Jeanette: That I could play a musical instrument, other than the recorder. I could play tunes like 'Go And Tell Aunt Nancy' on my recorder at Shaftesbury High. How mind-blowing is that?

Jackie: I had piano lessons and got to Grade 1. I went to Miss Fish at Iwerne Minster and then Mrs Pike at Twyford.

Jeanette: I suppose some other skills that we learnt at Shaftesbury High were sewing and cooking. And I was never very good at either of them, Jackie. To this day, I hate having to use a needle and thread and I really don't like the oven.

Jackie: The trouble was, at school, everything took so long, didn't it? It took an entire term to make an apron.

Jeanette: We had to keep pressing things. And why on earth did we have to use tacking stitches? They were sort of a guide to where we had to use the machine. Does anyone use tacking stitches today I wonder?

Jackie: Goodness knows.

Jeanette: You know what, Jackie? I'm now going to go off and find out the point of logarithms.

Jackie: Well, when you find out, Jeanette, let me know.

17

Go to Work on An Egg

'I was rather in love with him… but our eyes never met over the cabbages.'

Imagine a workplace where…
There are virtually no health and safety regulations.
Your job is to scrape broken eggs from the floor.
Plastic carrier bags are a thing of the future.
Barcodes and scanners don't exist.

Jeanette: Did you have a weekend job?

Jackie: Oh yes, I worked at International Stores, which, at that time was the main supermarket in Shaftesbury. It was on the corner of Mustons Lane and the High Street.

Jeanette: So, was it exciting?

Jackie: I worked there Friday evenings and Saturday mornings. I was in charge of weighing and labelling the cheese. It was wrapped in plastic film and passed to the deli counter.

Jeanette: Sounds very important work.

Jackie: Jeanette, I can still smell the burning plastic aroma that came from the cling film machine. The butchery manager, Mr Burt, sliced the cheese into blocks and I did the rest. I wore a fetching blue nylon overall, but I didn't wear protective gloves or head gear and the lethal bacon-slicing machine that lurked nearby, was devoid of any health and safety notices. It was all very gung-ho.

Jeanette: My first Saturday job was at the greengrocers, run by Mr and Mrs Welch, at 4 Church Lane on Shaftesbury High Street. I was paid 12/- (60p) for four hours. I still have the employment card, issued by Dorset Council in 1971, authorising me to work in the shop.

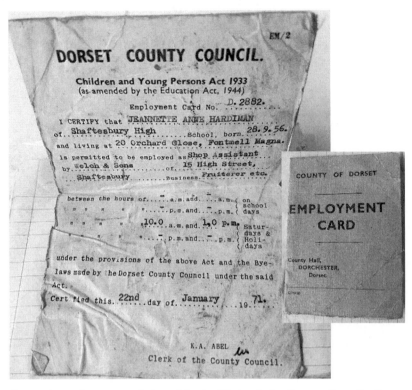

Jeanette's employment card, issued by be Clerk of the County Council, County Hall, Dorchester.

Jackie: What did you do there?

Jeanette: My first task of the day was to place trays of fruit and vegetables on the ledge, outside, in front of the shop window. It was quite common for greengrocers to do this to entice customers into the shop. Just across the road at 12 High Street, there was a rival greengrocer's shop called Robinson's and they displayed their goods in exactly the same way. They had a 'Saturday boy' who looked like the singer Cat Stevens. I was rather in love with him, and we were often setting out our displays at the same time, but our eyes never met over the cabbages.

Jackie: At least you had a romantic interest. Nothing like that cropped up at International Stores. I did some shelf-stacking, which I found strangely enjoyable; the art of 'facing up' the shelves probably satisfied my OCD tendencies.

Jeanette: Mr Welch took great pride in his produce, polishing his apples to achieve the highest possible gloss, discarding anything that was past its best and generally being very creative with his displays which were neat, eye-catching and colourful. And unlike today when everything is available all year round, these were the days when fruit and vegetables were only available in season, so it was still exciting to see and smell the first strawberries, peaches, peas or lettuce.

Jackie: And I bet there was no self-service.

Jeanette: Absolutely not. And there were no plastic carrier bags either. Purchases such as potatoes were often placed loose in the customer's own shopping bag. And brown paper bags, hanging on string around the shop, were used for items such as apples or pears.

Jackie: And now we've come full circle with recycling haven't we?

Jeanette: Yes, indeed we have. Also, I was working in the shop on 15th February 1971, also known as 'D Day' when the UK converted to decimal currency. At 14 years of age, I swiftly grasped the concept of decimals and found it astonishing that so many of the customers were struggling to get to grips with it.

Jackie: Did you work anywhere else at weekends?

Jeanette: My next weekend job was in Key Markets, at 36 High Street which, when it first opened, was considered very modern and a vast improvement on the seemingly outdated International Stores (sorry Jackie). The manager was Ernie Hoskins, who was very popular, and he and his family lived in the flat above the shop. It was staffed mainly by ladies, all wearing their yellow nylon overalls and little caps embellished with, unsurprisingly, a key.

Jackie: Oh, so like me, you also worked in a supermarket?

Jeanette: Yes, on Fridays, after school, from 5pm to 7pm, I'd be on the check-out. Unlike today where items are simply passed over the barcode scanner, prices needed to be keyed into the till. Over time I built up my speed on the keys as I became more experienced, tapping away as if I was using a typewriter. And because most people used cash in those days (computers, calculators and 'contactless' were yet to come) you had to manually calculate how much change was due to the customer.

Jackie: Goodness, you must have been good if you were allowed on the checkout.

Jeanette: On Saturday mornings, I was relegated to the aisles, labelling goods with a price-gun that spat out labels. And after sticking the labels on the tins or packets, I stacked them on the shelves. To this day, I hate removing any items from the shelf if a member of staff is trying to fill the display, because I know how annoyed I used to feel when somebody created a gap.

Did you have any other weekend jobs?

Jackie: I was a waitress at Milestones, a tearoom in Compton.

'MILESTONES'
Compton Abbas
SHAFTESBURY . DORSET

Old-World 17th-Century House in
own grounds.   Large Car Park.

3 miles South of Shaftesbury
on the A350 Road

Attractive Tea Room & Tea Garden.
Open Daily (except Thursdays),
for Morning Coffee and Afternoon
Dorset Cream Teas.
10 a.m. — 12.30 p.m.
3 p.m — 5.30 p.m.

Garden Chalet, 3 Bedrooms & Bathroom for Letting
B & B Only
Proprietor: Mrs. N. Smith
Telephone: Fontmell Magna 360

Jeanette: I think I tried to get a job there a few times, but they didn't seem interested.

Jackie: They were lovely old tea rooms, full of character with exposed stone walls and highly polished dark wood furniture. I think the place is a private residence now.

Jeanette: Was the money good?

Jackie: I think so and most of the customers were really generous tippers.

American visitors at Milestones tearooms in Compton Abbas in the 70s.

Jeanette: I guess it was all very traditional?

Jackie: Yes. Cream teas, with home-baked scones and proper loose-leaf tea, including Earl Grey. Everything was served on heavy white china. And the Farmhouse Tea featured a free-range boiled egg.

Jeanette: All sounds very lush.

Jackie: The boiled egg proved to be my nemesis as one day an egg cup wobbled so much on the tray, it landed in a diner's lap. I decided there and then that waitressing wasn't for me.

Jeanette: Well, funny you should mention eggs because another holiday job of mine was at Stonegate egg packing factory, located on Christy's Lane. Nadine Hipworth, my neighbour in Fontmell, worked there full-time and must have put a good word in for me. But in truth, it was a strange place, and I don't think I ever really fitted in properly.

Jackie: I can't quite picture you packing eggs Jeanette.

Jeanette: Eggs were loaded on to a conveyor belt and then passed through a dark booth where an infrared light indicated if there was a bad yolk or similar inside the shell. The operator in the booth rejected 'as necessary'. This was deemed to be a very important role and as holiday staff, I was never trusted or trained to do it.

Jackie: I can't believe they never trained you.

Jeanette: I don't think I was bothered at the time Jackie. But once successfully through the booth, the eggs trundled on down to a carousel where, depending on their weight, small, standard, large or extra-large, they'd trickle off the belt into the relevant section. Four of us stood around the carousel, waiting for the eggs to come our way at which point, we'd grab three in each hand and place them in an egg box. It took quite a lot of practice to be able to hold three eggs in each hand, particularly when they were large. However, after some time I managed to master it.

Jackie: Crikey. It sounds very technical.

Jeanette: One lady who worked there had the very exciting task of scraping up and collecting broken eggs from the floor. Then she placed them in a giant mixer, bottled the liquid and sent everything off somewhere where allegedly it was used in egg shampoo.

Jackie: Don't think I would have wanted her job.

Jeanette: And unbelievably, after slogging away all day, our final task before leaving was to scrub the floors around our stations.

Jackie: I don't suppose you wanted to work with eggs after that experience.

Jeanette: Jackie, if I learned one thing from the entire experience, it was that I never wanted to work in a factory.

18

Dressed To Impress

'The conductor had a ticket machine over one shoulder and a leather money bag over the other…. goodness knows how he managed to walk around.'

Imagine a time when…
Nurses wore white, puffy little armbands.
Every cinema had an usherette.
Postmen didn't wear shorts.
Bus conductors existed.

Jeanette: In the 60s and 70s, every bus had a conductor, working alongside the driver.

Jackie: Anyone who watched TV's 'On the Buses' will picture the scene, Reg Varney and his sidekick, both dressed in their uniforms, topped off with a peaked cap.

Jeanette: The conductor had a ticket machine over one shoulder and a leather money bag over the other, goodness knows how he managed to walk around. The ticket machine had a dial that could be turned to the appropriate fare amount, and made a strange little clicking noise as the ticket spilled out.

Jackie: Of course, there were no card payments, everything was strictly cash and we were trained to always have the correct money so that no change was required.

Jeanette: Oh yes, it was really frowned upon if you didn't have the right money.

Also, my mum constantly told me that I must hold on to the ticket, just in case the inspector boarded the bus and asked to see it.

Jackie: I don't think I ever saw an inspector, did you?

Jeanette: Never.

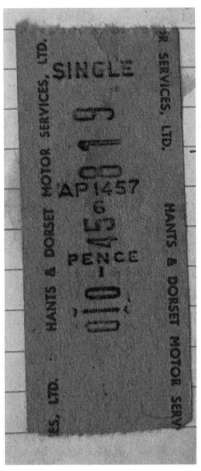

Do you remember travelling by bus, clutching your ticket in case an inspector asked for it?

This single bus ticket for the number 24 bus operating between Bournemouth and Shaftesbury, was issued by 'Hants & Dorset Motor Services Ltd'.

Jackie: Then there was the milkman, who drove an electric milk float.

Jeanette: Very ahead of its time.

Jackie: He delivered bottles of red, silver or gold top milk and wore a white coat with a stripy pinafore and a peaked cap. Think Benny Hill and 'Ernie.'

Jeanette: And there was the coalman.

Jackie: Quite often they wore those black donkey jackets with the shoulders reinforced with leather or pvc panels.

Jeanette: Even the postman wore a strict uniform in the 60s. They wouldn't have dreamt of wearing the shorts and fleeces that today's staff wear.

Jackie: Our postman wore a navy-blue jacket, trousers and a peaked cap. Think 'Postman Pat.'

Jeanette: And hospital staff look very different today, most of them wear scrubs, a much more practical option to the strict old-style uniforms.

Jackie: In the 60s, nurses wore an overall in a colour that denoted status. And a white pinafore, white cap and strange little puffy armbands.

Jeanette: Doctors wore white coats and there was a matron in charge of the hospital. That's another job that no longer exists.

Jackie: The matron ran the hospital with a 'rod of iron.' Lots of people still maintain that standards of cleanliness in modern-day hospitals are well below the standards that matron demanded.

Jeanette: What about the cinema? Anyone visiting was shown to their seat by the usherette who shone a torch to indicate empty seats.

Jackie: The Savoy Cinema in Shaftesbury always had an usherette who magically appeared in the interval to sell ice creams and orange juice. She wore a creamy yellow overall with a little cap and stood at the front of the theatre, underneath the screen, with her ice cream tray hanging on a thick strap from her neck.

Jeanette: And the office world has also seen tremendous changes.

Jackie: Dress code was really important in the office. When I worked at The Grosvenor, skirts had to be knee-length, hair tied back and certainly no cleavage.

Jeanette: And when I worked at Midland Bank, we had to wear tights. Bare legs weren't allowed.

Jackie: Well, all in all, uniforms were very important in the 60s and 70s.

Jeanette: Yes, but I must say, in many cases, I prefer today's more relaxed attitude.

19

Keeping Up Appearances

'What was 'shrink to fit' all about? You had to sit in the bath, in cold water,
wearing your jeans and they supposedly shrunk to your shape and size.'

Imagine…
Considering a bloomer suit to be your favourite outfit.
Bothering to repair laddered tights.
Wearing jeans in the bath.
Darning socks.

Jeanette: Did you have a mini skirt, Jackie?

Jackie: Yes. My favourite mini skirt had blue polka-dots.

Jeanette: Ooooh. My favourite was blue linen, with a very thin belt. I wore it with tights, which were quite new on the scene in the early 70s. Sometimes I wore white tights, often with a pattern down the side of the leg.

Jackie: Some of those white tights had holes down the side of the leg too.

Jeanette: They did. And of course, tights were very expensive. If you laddered a leg, you did your utmost to mend it. Sometimes you darned a ladder, or maybe put nail varnish on it to stop it running further. And in extreme cases, you cut off the bad leg and replaced it with a good leg from another pair of tights.

Jackie: I'm sure it wasn't cost-effective, but that's what we did. And of course, everyone wore petticoats and slips, didn't they?

Jeanette: My mum wore something called a roll-on. It had a bra, girdle and suspenders all built in. It was almost as though you got to a certain age and had to hold everything in.

Jeanette, her brother and cousins, smartly turned-out at 20 Orchard Close.

Jackie: It was like an early form of Spanx wasn't it? It must have been so uncomfortable. The days before everyone went to the gym and kept in shape. And talking of underwear, I often used to go to Chesterfield White in Shaftesbury and buy vests.

Jeanette: Oh, everyone wore a vest, didn't they?

Jackie: And Gran Hardiman used to buy her bloomers from there too. Pink or blue.

Jeanette: What was your first grown-up outfit?

Jackie: Well, one that sticks in my mind is my yellow smock top, which I wore with my brown Oxford bags and massive platform shoes.

Jeanette: Ah yes, I had some orange check Oxford bags. In fact, back then there were lots of checked patterns around. Things like Ben Sherman shirts which both girls and boys wore.

Jeanette's platform shoes, flared jeans and checked cheesecloth shirt.

Jackie: With the button-down collars and breast pocket.

Jeanette: Those shirts were often worn with a Trevira jacket and trousers or skirt. I think they were called tonic suits. The fabric was sort of iridescent. I had a blue tonic suit that I wore with white tights, brown 'granny' lace-up shoes and for some reason, a bunch of red plastic cherries on my lapel.

Jackie: That's right. It was a bit of a nod to the skinheads or the mods. Something like that.

Jeanette: Yes, Mum refused to buy me 'granny' lace-ups for ages. She said they were ugly. But I managed to get a pair in the end.

Jackie: Mind you, looking back, she wasn't wrong was she? They were pretty 'clumpy'.

Jeanette: I suppose you're right. But at the time, I thought they were great.

Jackie's favourite smock from Chelsea Girl and sister Sue in stripy jumpsuit.

A bit later in the 70s, I had a cheesecloth check shirt. It was in pinks and blues, and I loved it. In fact, I had a few cheesecloth shirts.

Jackie: Yes, cheesecloth was all the rage at one time.

Jeanette: The other outfit I loved was a bloomer suit, bought from Freemans catalogue. It had a zipped top with diagonal blue and white stripes, with dark blue bloomers. I thought I was the 'bees knees' in that outfit and I think I wore it to my very first dance at Shaftesbury Town Hall. How exciting.

Jackie: What about hot pants? I had some brown ones with a bib.

Jeanette: Mine were lilac, also with a bib. I wore them with tights and black, wet-look boots, which were more like close-fitting socks. My feet sweated terribly in them and probably stank. I also had a pair of red and white, wet-look shoes.

Jackie: I had a red, wet-look mac with a white zip down the front.

Jeanette: I always wanted a wet-look mac. But I think the fabric was PVC, wasn't it? Slightly stiffer and thicker than wet-look.

Jeanette in flowery maxi, floppy hat and platforms at a 70s wedding..

Jackie: You're probably right there. All I know is that it was really uncomfortable to wear.

Jeanette: I still have a photo of me at a wedding in the 70s. I'm wearing a maxi dress, big floppy hat and massive platform shoes.

Jackie: You wouldn't look out of place wearing that outfit now to be honest. But platform shoes were incredible. They were so high.

Jeanette: I think my mum used to wear them too. They were all the rage.

Jackie: And the higher the better. Pop stars like Elton John and David Bowie wore outrageous platform shoes and boots.

Jeanette: What about seersucker fabric? Did you like it?

Jackie: I had a blue and yellow seersucker blazer. They were very 'in' then weren't they, along with herringbone.

Jeanette: Herringbone, hugely inspired by Biba. I know I had a blue and black herringbone midi coat.

Jackie: And I know my sister had a purple, herringbone maxi coat which sadly got cut off to knee-length for me.

Jeanette: To be honest, you were either a 'maxi' or a 'midi' person. People didn't really mix the two.

Jackie: In the 70s, needlecord made a comeback. It was thinner than corduroy.

Jeanette: My very trendy neighbour Nadine, had some needlecord, drainpipe-style trousers. She was very tall and skinny and looked great in them. But they were quite a change from the flared style that we'd all been wearing for a while.

Flares and Scholl sandals in the early 70s.

Jackie: Bell-bottoms had been all the rage for a while in the late 60s.

Jeanette: I think that fraying the bottoms of your jeans was the thing to do.

Jackie: I suppose one of the earliest, fashionable shoes were flip-flops.

Jeanette: But they were so basic. Just rubber, with the wavy pattern on the thong and available in just a few colours.

Jackie: Yellow, green, blue and red. That was it. And they took ages to break in.

Checked blazers were all the rage in the 70s.

Jeanette: You'd end up with a plaster around the piece that went between your toes. The blisters could be agony.

Jackie: What about Scholls?

Jeanette: Oh yes. They were a sort of sophisticated flip-flop weren't they?

Jackie: And only sold at the chemist's shop.

Jeanette: There were lots of copies. But the genuine Dr Scholl's had that lovely metal buckle on the front.

Jackie: My first memorable pair of 'grown up' shoes were pink suede, with a tiny little heel and laces on the front. I wore them to a wedding with a red, bri-nylon suit.

Jeanette: Lovely. My first 'grown-up' shoes were blue, with a little heel and they tied at the front and had a bit of a hole. Then there were things like wedges and ankle strap shoes.

Jackie: I love an ankle strap.

Jeanette: And espadrilles. They've been around forever haven't they, Jackie?

Jackie: They're timeless really. What about boots?

Jeanette: My neighbour had a pair of beige, suede, over-the-knee boots. I loved them. But she also had long legs, which I didn't have.

Jackie: I think my sister had a very similar, purple pair.

Jeanette: That same neighbour, also had a pair of white, patent, lace up boots that I coveted.

Jackie: Very 'Nancy Sinatra'.

What about jeans? It was so important to be 'on brand'. Levi, Brutus or Wrangler were acceptable. If you didn't have one of those makes, you were laughed out of town.

Jeanette: My dad constantly encouraged me to consider buying jeans from supermarkets. Well, there wasn't a chance I was going to be seen dead in those.

Jackie: What about shrink to fit? What was that all about? You had to sit in the bath, in cold water, wearing your denim jeans and they supposedly shrunk to your shape and size.

Jeanette: It was absolutely ridiculous, but we did it. I also had a denim dress at one point.

Jackie: I had a denim skirt. But in the 60s, fabrics were very different to nowadays. Things like jeans didn't have any stretch in them.

Jeanette: And there were some horrible fabrics around. Things like Crimplene, rayon and nylon.

Jackie: All 'easy-dry' materials that I suppose helped out the busy housewives of the time.

Jeanette: Generally, you'd have to go to one of the bigger towns to find clothes. And it was a real treat, a day out and you saved hard beforehand. People didn't use credit or debit cards in those days. There were just cheques, or good old cash.

Jackie: We also bought lots of clothes from the catalogues, like Freemans or Empire Stores.

Jeanette in her red and white checked seersucker jacket.

Jeanette: We called them club books. I think Freemans was the most popular. It had people like Lulu modelling her own range of clothes.

Jackie: Everyone could pay weekly for things. You had your club card to keep track of things.

Jeanette: And when you ordered things, you so looked forward to receiving that massive parcel. Sadly, you often returned most of it. I suppose it was an early form of Amazon.

Jackie: Except you'd have to wait much longer for your parcel.

Jeanette: The word 'boutique' was new too. It signified that it was for younger people. I loved Chelsea Girl, it was all black and red.

And there were also Bus Stop and Top Shop in the early 70s. In Southampton we visited C&A.

Jackie: Apart from Hine and Parsons, there weren't many places to buy fashionable clothes in Shaftesbury were there?

Jeanette: One thing I used to buy from good old Hine and Parsons was a chiffon scarf. I collected them, in fact, I had every colour of the rainbow. I tied them around my neck and left the end flowing, or sometimes, I tied one around my waist, which was much smaller then. It really was the end of an era when Hine & Parsons closed its doors for the last time.

Jackie: I know, it was somewhere we visited many times growing up. It always had a certain distinctive smell that could whisk me back in time. I've never been quite sure what that certain smell was. Could it be the hundreds of rolls of fabric? Pretty Polly tights and old lady slippers? Tea towels and handkerchiefs?

Mum browsed through the massive pattern books, usually Simplicity, Butterick or McCalls, to find the template for that perfect shift or trouser suit.

Jeanette: It was quite an occasion going to choose a dress pattern. Did your mum go there before she made your sister's wedding dress?

Jackie: Yes, and our orange seersucker bridesmaid dresses started life in Hine & Parsons. I also had a classic little girl frock with a full skirt and a bow around the waist made from Sooty and Sweep fabric and a bright red smock mini dress and bloomers.

Jeanette: Your mum was a 'dab hand' with the sewing machine.

Jackie: I loved the 'swish' of the measuring tape and sound of the heavy scissors on the cutting tables, the choosing of the buttons on little slips of cardboard, the bias binding, the ribbon and hook and eye fasteners, all selected and taken home in a Hine and Parsons paper bag with its iconic pink and black logo.

Jeanette: Of course, the other haberdashery shop in the High Street was Cordery's. The name's still on the step where the entrance used to be at the lower end of the High Street. There was also an iron gate in the entrance to the alley way, which was closed at night.

The A. Cordery name remains at the entrance
to the former shop in Shaftesbury High Street.

Jackie: I can see generously proportioned Mr Cordery now, in a three-piece suit and little round spectacles, standing there in the shop doorway.

Jeanette: Cordery's was also the stockist for our school uniform. You went up the stairs, out the back and spent a fortune.

Jackie: There was no straying from the official uniform. Shoes had to be the regulation colour, style, and heel height and these were the days when shoes were repaired rather than thrown away. It was a trip to Mr Reynolds, the shoe repairer in Shaftesbury, if shoes needed a new sole or heel. The smell of the glue and leather is another rare and evocative aroma which transports me back to the 60s.

Jeanette: We went to Hine & Parsons or Cordery's for wool as well because Mum and Nan were always knitting. Jumpers for the children but also sweaters for my dad. When I was at Fontmell Primary School Mum knitted me a 'false' polo neck to wear under a V-neck jumper.

Jackie: The peaceful sound of the click of knitting needles reminds me of my mum pulling wool from a ball with the cat having a tug of war with it at her feet.

Jeanette: My nan often knitted socks and she taught me how to darn them too.

Jeanette's button-down shirt on show for her employment card.

Jackie: Nobody considered throwing socks away, it was make do and mend all the way!

Jeanette: She used one of those little wooden mushroom-shaped things when she was darning.

Jackie: As well as buying material and running up a new dress on her Singer treadle sewing machine, Mum refashioned her own or my big sister's outgrown clothes for me to wear. Her own wedding dress was cut down and made into a special dress for me to wear to Salisbury Cathedral for a church event.

Jeanette: Waste not, want not.

Jackie: The most extreme 'recycling' must be when she refashioned a pair of bright orange curtains into a flared trousers and waistcoat combo for an 11-year-old me. Upholstery didn't faze Mum either and chairs and sofas often had a new lease of life under her expert hands.

Jeanette: Every home had a button box or tin containing hundreds, if not thousands, of buttons of all sizes, shapes, and colours.

Mum fashioned an orange trouser suit from a pair of old curtains for Jackie.

Jackie: The button tin provided hours of fun. I loved finding the gilt military-style buttons or tiny baby buttons in the shape of bunnies or teddy bears.

Jeanette: When Mum sadly passed away, I gave her button tin away, which I so regret.

Jackie: Recycling is a word which wasn't heard at all in the 60s but, looking back, my mother was the absolute queen of recycling and up-cycling.

Jeanette: Yes, she was quite a legend in that field. Sadly, we live in such a throwaway society now. If your mum was still alive, she could have launched her own podcast and called it 'Winnie's Country Ways'.

Jackie: Great title. My mum was certainly ahead of her time.

Jeanette: Well, I think they say that if you can remember the 60s you weren't there but, do you know what, I think we're the exception!

20

Looking Good

'You spat on the cake of black mascara and then rubbed it with the little brush, it was a bit like a tiny dustpan and brush...'

Imagine...
Washing your hair over the sink using a tap attachment.
Creating hair conditioner from raw eggs and lemon.
Backcombing your hair into a beehive hairstyle.
Spitting on your mascara.

Jeanette: In the hairdressing salon, everyone sat in a row, wearing rollers and a hair net, under those hooded hairdryers. I don't think the blow-dry had been invented!

Jackie: Nowadays, you're lucky if you find one of those old driers in a salon. I think they're hidden away, covered in cobwebs.

Jeanette: There was always a certain smell in the hairdressing salon wasn't there? I suppose it was hair spray, which came in massive aerosol cans.

Jackie: Yes, always lashings of hairspray! Salons don't smell like that now.

Jeanette: Seemed though, in the 60s, everyone came out of the hairdresser's looking the same. It was either a shampoo and set, or a perm. People didn't go to the hairdressers very often. Only on special occasions.

Jackie: My mum cut my hair until I was about seven. It was so long; I could sit on it and I hated having it washed and combed. There were so many tangles. And I don't think we used conditioner.

Jeanette: I think we made our own. A concoction of raw eggs and lemon springs to mind. And occasionally, I'd add some vinegar to my final rinse to bring out the highlights in my hair.

Jackie: I know Mum used to perm Gran Hardiman's hair at home with that awful stuff that smelt so strong. I think it had ammonia in it. And she used those very tiny perm curlers.

Jeanette: I think it was called Twink. My mum used it at some point too.

Jackie: That's right. It was a home perming kit.

Jeanette: My first experience of a perm was in the early 70s when I had my lovely long hair cut off and styled into a 'Farrah Fawcett' cut, all flicked out at the edges. The first time I washed and dried it myself, I used one of those rounded blow-dry brushes and it got stuck in my hair. Eventually I had to cut it out.

Jackie: Oh no, what a disaster. Farrah Fawcett was beautiful, wasn't she? She was one of TV's 'Charlie's Angels'.

Jeanette: She was gorgeous, but I didn't look much like her. I don't like perms and won't be having another one any time soon.

Jackie: I've had several curly perms over the years. Goodness knows what damage they've done to my hair.

Jeanette: I've had several dreadful hairstyles over the years, reflected in those awful school photos that parents and grandparents used to have on show.

Jackie: When I was young and my hair was very long, I often wore it in two plaits, or maybe bunches.

Jeanette: Me too. Sometimes I had a little bun on the top of my head. I think it was called a chignon. Mum wrapped my hair around a sort of doughnut. And of course, I always had ribbons in my hair, often to match what I was wearing.

Jackie: Anyway, eventually I got a 'pageboy' cut.

Jeanette: Was it like Purdy in The New Avengers?

Jackie: No, it was more like a basin cut.

Jeanette: Oh dear. That's a shame.

Jackie: Let's just say that I didn't look much like the gorgeous Joanna Lumley, who played Purdy.

Jackie rocking a 70s curly perm.

Jeanette: So many pop stars and actresses influenced hairstyles in the 60s and 70s. Like Sandie Shaw and her bob.

Jackie: She always sang in bare feet. I'm not quite sure why.

Jeanette: Me neither. But there was also Cilla Black who started off with a bob and then got it cut shorter.

Jackie: And Kathy Kirby, who had her hair flicked outwards.

Jeanette: She also always had very shiny lips. I was fascinated by them. Probably just lip gloss, but she was famous for those lips. In fact, I'm convinced that's where I got my love of lipstick from.

Jackie: What about Dusty Springfield? She usually had a beehive and loads of dark eye makeup.

Jeanette: Oh, the beehive. People backcombed like mad and once you had everything in place, you could poke here and there with a tail comb until you had it at the correct height.

Jackie: We had a neighbour who backcombed her hair within an inch of its life till it was really high. She must have used gallons of hairspray on it.

Jeanette: Elnett hairspray was around then. That was the posh one really. There were most probably some cheaper brands available like Supersoft or Silvikrin.

Jeanette: By the time I started work at Midland Bank, Shaftesbury in 1973, my hair was long and poker straight again, which was the fashion around that time.

Jackie: What about feather cuts? They were all the rage in the 70s. Your hair was razor-cut at the bottom and hung like tendrils around your neck.

Jeanette: You had to have a certain kind of hair for a feather cut to work well. There was a girl at Shaftesbury High School who had really wavy hair in an old-fashioned style. But once she got a feather cut she never looked back. It really suited her.

Jackie: What was going on with men's hair Jeanette? In the mid-60s, I suppose the Beatle cut was big.

Jeanette: But even though their hair was fairly short, my dad always referred to them as 'long-haired louts'. I dread to think what he thought about The Rolling Stones.

Jackie: Brylcreem was still popular, mostly with older men who slicked their hair back. Left over from the 50s I suppose. And of course, Cliff Richard and Elvis had a quiff.

Jeanette: Then in the 70s, came the mullet from Rod Stewart and Kevin Keegan's 'man perm'.

Jackie: Usually the 'man perm' came with a matching moustache.

Jeanette: What about shampoo? I mean, we didn't have the choice we have now did we?

Jackie: We were very restricted. There was Vosene. That was dark green and medicated. You used it if you had dandruff.

Jeanette: My absolute favourite was Silvikrin Lemon and Lime. It was especially for greasy hair and as a teenager, my hair was very greasy. I also liked Supersoft and Sunsilk.

Jackie: Very often we bought shampoo in small sachets, probably because we didn't wash our hair as much in those days. And of course, washing our hair was an ordeal. We didn't have showers then, so you'd wash your hair over the sink or bath using one of those rubber hose tap attachments.

Jeanette: Usually, one side of the attachment flew off the tap half way through a hair wash so not only were you sprayed with hot or cold water, but you also had to re-attach everything whilst having a head full of foam. And trying to get the temperature right was a nightmare too.

Jackie: What about colouring your hair? I think the first time I coloured mine, cousin Flora did it for me and it was pure peroxide. My hair was practically white.

Jeanette: Sometimes I used something called Hint of a Tint, by Inecto which was really a very subtle dye. Then, later on, I often used henna to add red highlights. It was a powder and smelt awful, but it was natural.

Jackie: There was a similar tint for blondes called 'Sun In'.

Jeanette: What about drying your hair? I think our first hairdryer was a Morphy Richards. It was pink and probably only had two settings, hot and cold. Every so often my hair caught in the fan and there was a horrible burning smell.

Jackie: Pifco was also a popular make and there were the ones with a shoulder strap and a plastic hat attachment, which was basically a shower cap, so you could walk around while you were drying your hair. Revolutionary.

Jeanette: State of the art I'd say. Did you ever use heated rollers?

Jackie: Oh yes, of course. I think I had some Clairol ones. Carmen was another big name. And they worked a treat, although I often stuck one of the spiky hair grips into my head.

Jeanette: I had some curling tongs. But I often got into a bit of a pickle with them. I wound my hair the wrong way around the barrel and ended up with a huge dent. I was always forgetting to switch them off and leaving them on the carpet. I singed the carpet countless times, so I hate to think what they were doing to my hair.

Jackie: Not really up to the standard of today's hair straighteners.

Jeanette: What's been your favourite hairstyle over the years?

Jackie: Definitely not the Purdy basin cut, Jeanette.

Jeanette: And mine was definitely not the 'Farrah Fawcett'.

Jackie: What about make up? There wasn't so much choice back then was there?

Jeanette: There were far fewer brands, although I guess that because we were younger, we tended to use the cheaper makes. Rimmel, Outdoor Girl and Miners spring to mind first.

Jackie: Miners was turquoise and black packaging, wasn't it?

Jeanette: Yes, very distinctive. And in particular, the mascara was very popular. It was like a small compact with a cake of black mascara, rather like a cake of paint.

Jackie: And you had to spit on the cake of black mascara and then rub it with the little brush. In fact, it was a bit like a tiny dustpan and brush, wasn't it?

Jeanette: Rimmel's most popular product was probably 'Hide and Heal' concealer. As a spotty teenager, I had it dotted all over my face to hide everything.

Jackie: I think it only came in two colours; light or dark.

Jeanette: Eyeliner was very popular too. I sometimes used a liquid, peel-off one. I looked forward to taking it off, hopefully in one long strip. Very satisfying.

Jackie: My big sister often wore false eyelashes. Lip gloss was all the rage too. You put it over your lipstick.

Jeanette: Lipstick was very matt and back then it came in two sizes. The big size came in a swivel case and there was a smaller size which came with a push-up mechanism. Made sense I suppose, if you couldn't afford the bigger size.

Jackie: And as the 70s rolled on, purples and plums were popular.

Jeanette: That was Biba. Everyone looked very tired, like they were sleep-deprived.

Many ladies had a powder compact in their handbag.

Jackie: Most ladies carried a powder compact.

Jeanette: That's right. In fact, I used to collect powder compacts. I still have some at home. Big makes like Kigu and Stratton were very popular. People used either solid face powder or loose. In fact, Ponds made a loose powder, packaged in a little, round cardboard box. There was a seal on the box and the moment it was broken, the powder went everywhere.

Jeanette: We called perfume scent didn't we? Evening in Paris came in a dark blue bottle and for a long time was the only scent around. Mum also had a bottle of lavender water.

Jackie: My mum had a little bottle of 4711 cologne on her dressing table and Dad always had Old Spice in the cream coloured bottle with a stopper.

Jeanette: Nan Sims wore 4711, the little bottles were cute. There was Coty L'Aimant which was pink and came in a black ceramic bottle with a dipper. I loved old-fashioned scents like Ashes of Roses and Lily of the Valley.

Jackie: The smell of Charlie perfume and Brut after shave are both reminders of the 70s. Musk was popular too, I think it was meant to make you irresistible to the opposite sex!

Jackie: But overall, there wasn't an obsession with looking young was there?

Jeanette: No. Things like face lifts were for the rich and famous. And there were no beauty salons or nail bars were there Jackie?

Jackie: No. We did everything at home.

Jeanette: All in all though, considering our younger days, we're not doing too bad in the beauty stakes.

21

A Touch of Bling

'I always loved those charms with banknotes inside. There was a ten-shilling note, a £1 note and a £5 note. So useful to have if you ever got short of money.'

Imagine...
Having banknotes hanging from your charm bracelet.
Using cigarette coupons to buy jewellery.
Buying earrings from Woolworths.
Owning a wind-up watch.

Jeanette: The very first piece of jewellery I wanted, was one of those little silver christening bracelets. They were adjustable, with a safety chain and were often engraved.

Jackie: Yes, everyone had one.

Jeanette: I didn't.

Jackie: No. Neither did I.

Jeanette: I wanted one. You could expand them as you grew up.

Jackie: What bracelets *did* you have?

Jeanette: Well, the first one was when I was very little, and I think Nan bought it for me. It was a collection of plastic, pastel-coloured beads and fake pearls on elastic. I think it was called a sweetheart bracelet. I loved it.

Jackie: Ah yes. I know what you mean. I used to read a comic called *Twinkle* that often came with a free plastic bracelet with coloured beads.

Snake bracelets were popular.

Jeanette: Snake bangles fascinated me. They often had coloured gems as the snake's eyes. Mind you, I didn't have one of those either.

Jackie: No, neither did I. But on my 18th birthday, I was given a charm bracelet.

Charms for bracelets were popular for birthday and Christmas gifts.

Jeanette: I always wanted one of those. And I bet yours was an original, really heavy with all the wonderful charms dangling down. Not like modern ones. A friend of mine had a fabulous silver one and I just adored the jangling sound it made when she moved around.

Jackie: I had a range of charms, people often gave them to me for birthdays and at Christmas, so I guess that solved a problem for everyone for a few years.

Jeanette: I always loved those charms with banknotes inside. There was a 10-shilling note, a £1 note and a £5 note. So useful to have if you ever got short of money.

Jackie: My favourite charm was a disc that you spun and it read 'Good Luck'. A sort of early fidget spinner I suppose.

Jeanette: What about those gate bracelets Jackie? They were pretty popular for a while. I know my mum had a gold one.

Jackie: They were fashionable in the late 70s. And there were also the padlock bracelets that had a safety chain. Always a sign of an expensive piece of jewellery.

I loved looking at the jewellery in the Marshall Ward catalogue. One thing I always wanted was a ring watch.

Jeanette: I actually had one of those. In the late 60s, early 70s, our French teacher at Shaftesbury High School wore one. She was very trendy, in fact she looked a bit like that singer Nana Mouskouri. I was fascinated every time she lifted her finger to check the time. I begged Mum and Dad for a ring watch and they bought me one for Christmas.

Aunty Joan's 60s bracelet watch.

Jackie: What was your first wristwatch like?

Jeanette: It was a Timex, very plain face with a blue fabric strap. It came with a free china Cinderella ornament which I think I probably liked more than the watch. I kept that ornament for years.

Jackie: And then, in the 70s, lots of big, colourful watches started to appear.

Jeanette: I had a lovely watch with a square, red face.

Jackie: All those watches had a wind-up mechanism. It wasn't until probably the mid 70s that battery and digital watches made by firms like Casio, started to appear. I had a lovely battery watch with the sun and moon on the face and they moved throughout the day.

Jeanette: As a child, I spent ages in Woolworths looking at their collection of dress jewellery. I particularly loved the rings, all massive and set with fake stones. I'm sure if I saw them now I'd think they were ghastly. But at the time I was fascinated by them. They were displayed in glass-fronted cases on the counter.

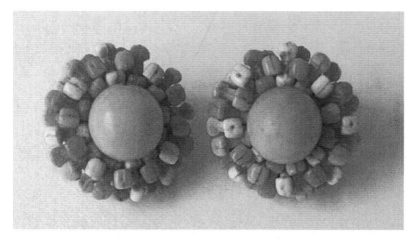

Plastic flower clip-on earrings.

Jackie: And then of course there were the earrings. My mum didn't have pierced ears so always wore clip-ons. I don't know how she did it, they were so uncomfortable.

Jeanette: I bet she could never wear them all day, probably only for special occasions. My nan always wore clip-ons too and we were always finding an odd earring down the side of a chair, or on the floor.

Jackie: In the 60s, my big sister wore those big, hooped, plastic earrings. And she also had some huge daisy earrings.

Jeanette: Woolworths sold those big, hooped, plastic 60s style ones, some monochrome, some in pastel shades.

Jackie: When did you get your ears pierced Jeanette?

Jeanette: I was 16 and had a holiday job at Stonegate egg-packing factory on Christy's Lane. I got my first pay-packet and tore down the road to Allum's the jewellers to get them done. I don't think I've gone a day without earrings since then.

Jackie: Yes, that's where I got mine pierced, but I found it quite traumatic.

Jeanette: Did you? I thought it was all really exhilarating.

Jackie: Obviously you must have a higher pain threshold than me. Then, after the trauma of having it done, we had to wear sleepers, turning them constantly and bathing our ears in surgical spirit.

Jeanette: Aunty Jean was one of the first people I knew to have her ears pierced. I can see her now with lovely little dangly earrings and I vowed then that I'd get it done as soon as I could.

Jackie: In the late 70s, I think boys started to have their ears pierced too, but only in one ear.

Jeanette: I don't think I would have gone out with anyone wearing an earring. Bit too radical for me. I did have some lovely gold wedding ring earrings that Aunty Joan got me with her cigarette coupons.

 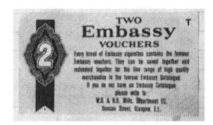

Jackie: My goodness, she must have smoked a lot to get you things with those coupons.

Jeanette: It was quite normal to smoke constantly.

Jackie: What about big gold hoops? They were so popular in the 70s, weren't they?

Jeanette: They're still around today.

Jackie: A sort of classic style really. Can't go wrong with a gold hoop.

Jeanette: And thinking about necklaces, you couldn't go wrong with a St Christopher in the 60s could you? Or a cross.

Jackie: You could give either as christening gifts. Or if you were a bridesmaid, you were often given either a silver cross or even a locket.

Jeanette: I still have the little gold locket that Mum and Dad gave me one Christmas. I think it was the first 'grown up' piece of jewellery I owned. I lost it one night, outside the Royal Chase Hotel and I returned the next day and found it in the leaves on the ground. I've kept it safe ever since.

A gold locket – Jeanette's first grown-up piece of jewellery.

Jackie: What about chokers? They were around in the 70s, weren't they?

Jeanette: I made my own from a strip of black velvet with one of my nan's brooches pinned to it. I wore it with a long black maxi skirt.

Jackie: Sounds very 'hip'.

Jeanette: It was. And there was also a time when it was fashionable to wear a sort of leather shoelace either around your neck, or your wrist.

Jackie: Sounds like something a cowboy might wear Jeanette.

Jeanette: What about the ingot? Gold or silver, which you'd wear on a chain.

Jackie: And worth their weight in gold or silver I suppose. Bit like sovereigns, which I never liked. Far too big and ostentatious. There were a lot of them in the club book too.

Jeanette: And brooches? My nan was never without one. She had a big collection, including one of those really weird furry bird claws, embellished with a massive fake stone. I was fascinated by it. I like a brooch though, don't you?

Jackie: Well, I think it's how you wear it that matters isn't it?

Jeanette: Yes, I still wear a brooch every so often. Very stylish.

Jackie: These days we don't always get the chance to wear lots of classic jewellery do we?

Jeanette: Maybe we should get some of those precious old pieces out on show.

22
Working Girls

'Offices were still very much a man's world'.

Imagine working for a company where…
You enter a beauty contest wearing an overall.
Desktop computers don't exist.
All bank managers are male.
All secretaries are female.

Jeanette: Your first full time job was in The Grosvenor Hotel in Shaftesbury wasn't it, Jackie?

Jackie: Yes, I began working there in 1977 when unemployment was high and so, even though I was a newly qualified secretary, I took a job as a chambermaid.

Jeanette: I bet it was hard work.

Jackie: It was hard physical work. I hauled the used sheets and towels in a huge laundry bag back to the Linen Room which was bulging with packs of plastic-wrapped freshly laundered sheets and towels.

Jeanette: And did you have to clean all the rooms, every day?

Jackie: I was given my quota of rooms by Betty the housekeeper who ran a pretty tight ship in those days. If my room list included 'stays' I'd feel elated as it meant the bed wouldn't need to be changed while 'departures' meant stripping beds, replenishing towels and cleaning thoroughly. Woe betide you if you didn't move furniture to vacuum and a tissue, or worse, was found lurking.

Jeanette: And I guess you didn't have lots of the time-saving gadgets and equipment that makes life easier now.

Jackie: That's right. For instance, it was still sheets and blankets then, duvets weren't in widespread use, so I was shown how to negotiate 'hospital corners' when making up the beds.

Jeanette: Gosh, a bit like working in a hospital really. But the rooms at The Grosvenor must have been 'top notch' because it was very exclusive wasn't it?

Jackie: Tea and coffee-making facilities were in every room along with writing paper and tiny bars of soap which had to be artistically arranged in the en suite bathrooms.

Jeanette: Wasn't that wonderful Chevy Chase sideboard still in The Grosvenor in the 70s?

Jackie: Yes, it was carved from a single block of oak. I've got fond memories of flicking a duster around the intricate carvings that depicted hunting scenes from the ancient ballad of Chevy Chase. It was a sad day when it was sold off to an American buyer by the hotel's owners in 2001. Apparently, it only narrowly survived Hurricane Katrina while in storage in New Orleans.

Jeanette: It was in a large room upstairs in the hotel, wasn't it?

Jackie: It was and that was where we spent our very welcome morning coffee break. We could 'people watch' from the first floor window and indulge in a spot of gossip while the residents of Shaftesbury went about their day.

Jeanette: The Grosvenor is supposedly haunted, isn't it?

Jackie: So they say. Although I didn't see any ghosts myself, several of my colleagues had. There was a 'dumb waiter' in the staff kitchen on the first floor and the 'Grey Lady' had appeared in the shaft there which was used to send breakfast trays from the kitchen to the bedrooms.

Jeanette: Were there many famous guests who stayed there?

Jackie: French crooner Sacha Distel came to stay and the Two Ronnies. At that time, they were huge stars and stayed at the hotel when filming their Charley Farley and Piggy Malone sketches.

Ronnie Barker was given the honeymoon suite with a four-poster bed. Not sure if that was because he was the boss in the comedy

The Chevy Chase sideboard was a central feature in the Grosvenor Hotel.

partnership or whether it was because he was about four times the size of Mr Corbett.

Jeanette: Does anything memorable stick out in your mind about your time working there?

Jackie: My workmates encouraged me to take part in Miss Catering 1978 and, while the majority of the entrants wore smart front of house suits with flattering scarves or slightly saucy waitress and lacy pinny ensembles, I was stuck in a less than flattering overall. Ever entered a beauty contest wearing an overall? Well, let me tell you it doesn't really increase your chances of success.

Jeanette: Oh, Jackie, that's just plain cruel.

'Miss Overall' Jackie, back third left, at Miss Catering 1978.

Jackie: Needless to say, I didn't make the grade, but happily I eventually swapped my 'Mrs Mop' outfit for a smart uniform as I was offered a job in the hotel reception with lovely head receptionist Phyllis.

Jeanette: So, you moved up in the world!

Jackie: I suppose you could say that, although a manual typewriter and old-style cord and plug switchboard were the only modern equipment in reception. I typed up the day's menus, checked hotel guests in and out and answered the phone. They paid with cash, cheque with a bank card or, if they were a little more flush, an American Express or Diners Club credit card. There was an art to using the pull across card machine when taking payment with one of those cards and with three copies of the receipt to deal with it was all a bit fiddly compared to today's contactless payments.

Jeanette: It was a bit like that in our office, everything was very manual.

Jackie: Of course, you worked just across the road in what was then Midland Bank.

The view from the Chevy Chase Lounge (latterly the Assembly Room) at the Grosvenor Hotel.

Jeanette: That's right. I started work there on 3rd December 1973. And before actually setting foot in the Shaftesbury branch, I attended a four-week induction course in the Southampton training centre, so I knew the basics of my role as a junior. Nevertheless, it was extremely daunting to ring the doorbell for the first time and embark on what turned out to be a 38-year career in banking.

Jackie: And banks were very staid and stiff in those days, weren't they?

Jeanette: Oh, yes. The office was furnished with massive wooden desks, dark wooden panelled walls, a locked door and screen between the counter and the back office and of course, absolutely none of the self-service equipment that's now commonplace.

Jackie: Banks were really quite imposing then.

Jeanette: These were the days when the bank manager was a very well-respected and important member of the community and at Christmas, gifts such as a brace of pheasant, rabbits, bottles of sherry and wine, chocolates and cakes flooded in for him. Invariably he'd take his pick of the better offerings and leave the staff to fight it out for the crumbs.

Jackie: Offices were still very much a 'man's world'.

Jeanette: Most, if not all senior management were male and ladies were expected to dress conservatively. No cleavage was permitted to be on show, no trousers, no bare legs, dresses and skirts a sensible length and hair and make-up neat and tidy.

Jackie: It was very much like that in The Grosvenor too. Secretaries were always female.

Jeanette: The bank manager always had a female secretary who took shorthand, typed up his letters and generally pandered to his every whim. The manual typewriter later changed to an electric typewriter, followed by word-processors and eventually computers.

Jeanette's wooden cashier's box from Midland Bank.

Jackie: Working in a bank was always seen to be a very good career choice though.

Jeanette: Everyone started at the bottom. As the newest member of staff, I was treated as the 'lowest of the low'. I was the office junior and duties included making morning coffee for everyone, which I had down to a fine art.

Jeanette's wooden calendar from Midland Bank.

I left the saucepan of milk warming up on the Baby Belling and quickly ran around the town delivering letters to other banks before returning to make the coffee just in time, before the milk scalded and boiled over. Perfect.

Jackie: You still make a mean cup of coffee, Jeanette.

Jeanette: It was also my job to guard the pavement area directly outside the building when the bullion van, staffed with guards, came to collect cash from the branch. I had to keep watch for robbers, armed with just a truncheon and a whistle. Goodness knows what would have happened if the guards had been attacked.

Jackie: But like the office in The Grosvenor, I suppose there were no computers.

Jeanette: Just before I started working there, a massive computer had been installed in the branch. The day's credits and debits were manually 'posted' to the central system via this computer, along with all new accounts, standing orders and other customers' amendments. There was a massive golf-ball printer on the computer that clattered throughout the day. By today's standards it was archaic, but this was the very start of automation in the bank.

Jackie: So there was just one big computer in the office?

Jeanette: That's right. There were no desk-top computers. In fact, there were no photocopiers or fax machines either. They were all things of the future. When I saw a fax machine in action for the first time, I thought it was magic.

Jackie: Laughable, isn't it? And now, fax machines are a thing of the past too.

Jeanette: Well, eventually, I worked my way up to cashiering. To many customers, this was a sign of success and ironically, no matter whatever else I ever managed to do in my banking career, my mother perceived being 'on the front' as my greatest achievement. Personally, I hated it and was probably one of the worst cashiers ever. Invariably I couldn't balance my till at the end of the day and because everyone was expected to balance 'to the penny' I spent hours searching for my differences. It wasn't one of my more enjoyable roles.

Jackie: Overall though, did you enjoy your time working there?

Jeanette: I suppose I enjoyed most of it although I'm sure today's young people wouldn't tolerate the treatment inflicted on the office junior and would challenge the status quo. But I'd been brought up to respect my elders and to follow instructions without questioning.

Jackie: How long did you work at Midland Bank in Shaftesbury?

Jeanette: About six years and then I had the opportunity to transfer to Jersey for a two-year contract. I was summoned to head office in Southampton to be interviewed by Miss Rose, the 'ladies' area personnel officer. I sped up the M27 to Southampton in my little white Mini and prepared to be 'screened' by Miss Rose who warned me, in a very stern manner, that because Jersey was awash with alcohol and hedonism, she'd be keeping a close eye on me and would bring me back home if I misbehaved. Needless to say, at 21 years of age, her words made me even more determined to take up the post.

Jackie: So you left Shaftesbury?

Jeanette: You couldn't see me for dust.

23

Name That Tune

'Big sister always bagged Paul and she kept a framed photo of him next to her bed. I had to be content with George!'

Imagine a time when…
The Beatles are considered to be 'long haired louts'.
Radio Luxembourg only aired in the evenings.
Music is only available on vinyl records.
Most girls belong to a fan club.

Jackie: I was watching musicals' week on Strictly Come Dancing the other day and one of the songs took me right back to my 60s childhood. Who could forget 'Flash Bang Wallop - what a picture!'

Jeanette: I think it was Tommy Steele who sang it wasn't it? From the musical *Half a Sixpence*.

Jackie: That's right. But I suppose our earliest memories are little rhymes like 'Round and round the garden' and 'Incy wincy spider'?

Jeanette: Yes and 'Ring o'ring o'roses' and 'Lucy Locket'. I think the first pop song I heard and really loved on the wireless was 'Bobby's Girl' by Susan Maughan and my dad always insisted it was my favourite song.

Jackie: I loved 'My Boy Lollipop' by a singer called Millie. I even had a little doll which I named Millie after I saw her on TV.

Jeanette: There were lots of comedy songs around before pop music really took hold. I have an early memory of listening to 'There's a Hole in My Bucket' by Harry Belafonte. I was fascinated how the song came full circle back to '…but there's a hole in my bucket'.

Jackie: I know what you mean. it's like 'Four Wheels on My Wagon' which was a popular pick on Junior Choice, which I think started on the 'Light' programme and was hosted by Ed 'Stewpot' Stewart.

Jeanette: I think Leslie Crowther was the very first presenter.

Jackie: They played all the classics; 'Puff the Magic Dragon', 'Swinging on a Star', 'Old Amsterdam... I saw a little mouse on the stair, a little mouse with clogs on', 'Right Said Fred'. And on Sunday lunchtimes we always listened to Two-Way Family Favourites.

Jeanette: It had a similar playlist; 'Little White Bull', 'Wonderful, Wonderful Copenhagen', 'Tulips from Amsterdam', 'Que Sera Sera' and 'The Deadwood Stage' by Doris Day, 'Mud, Mud, Glorious Mud', they were all sort of pre-pop songs really.

Jackie: At school, I loved singing in 'rounds' with songs like 'London's Burning' and 'Frère Jacques'. And the song 'Oranges and Lemons' had quite a dark connotation I believe, and we acted out the head chopping at school.

Jeanette: Our school hymn at Shaftesbury High was 'Jerusalem' which we always sang at the end of term.

Jackie: I think you're right. What about your earliest memories of music in the home? I think we actually had an old-style gramophone early on which played 78s and a radiogram a bit later before 'music centres' came in in the 70s. It had a smoked glass cover and we thought it was state-of-the-art. Mum and Dad played records by people like Mantovani.

Jeanette: My nan who lived on Gold Hill loved Jim Reeves singing 'Distant Drums'.

Jackie: That reminds me of visiting Aunty Peggy on a Sunday teatime because Uncle Maurice always played music by Jim Reeves. 'Apache' by The Shadows always reminds me of childhood holidays. And Mum loved 'The Carnival is Over' by The Seekers and also '24 hours from Tulsa' by Gene Pitney.

Jeanette: Grandad Sims loved 'Green Green Grass of Home' by Tom Jones. He didn't like much, but he liked that song. I think one of my brother's first records after he got a Dansette record player, was Stevie Wonder's 'For Once in My Life'.

Jackie: 'Dock of the Bay' by Otis Redding reminds me of taking my sister back to college in Poole on Sunday afternoon. Another 60s hit I love is 'Downtown' by Petula Clark.

Jeanette: 'Blockbuster' by Sweet makes me think of an old friend who was crazy about lead singer Bryan Connelly with his really long blonde hair.

Jackie: There was a girl at school who was mad about Leo Sayer, so I'm always reminded of her when I see or hear him.

I've got a good selection of vinyl 45s from the 70s; David Bowie, T Rex, Mott the Hoople, Bay City Rollers, David Cassidy, Slade, Queen. It's quite nostalgic to play them in the old-fashioned way on a turntable and hear those little 'crackles'.

Jeanette: The first time I heard 'Don't Cry For Me Argentina' by Julie Covington stays with me. We had no idea how big it would become. And when a friend played 'Stairway to Heaven' by Led Zeppelin, I thought it was fab.

Jackie: It seems amazing that pop stars from our childhood, such as Paul McCartney and Mick Jagger have had such long and successful careers. I don't think we imagined they'd last so long.

Jeanette: And what are your earliest memories of bands like The Beatles?

Jackie: Well, having a sister who was a teenager in the 60s meant I was exposed to the world of pop from an early age. We fought over which Beatle we could have! Big sister always bagged Paul and she kept a framed photo of him next to her bed. I had to be content with George!

Jeanette: Nobody ever wanted Ringo though.

Jackie: I wish I'd kept some of the Beatles memorabilia I had in the 60s. I've got vivid memories of a small pink guitar decorated with images of the fab four which I was given, aged five, as a gift when I was in Odstock Hospital in Salisbury having my tonsils out.

Jeanette: My dad called The Beatles 'long haired louts'. I went to the cinema with him though to see both *A Hard Day's Night* and *Help*. You either liked The Beatles or The Rolling Stones, didn't you?

Jackie: The Stones were the bad boys. My sister saw both The Beatles and The Rolling Stones in Bournemouth, probably at the Winter Gardens. My earliest memory of a pop concert was when Billy J Kramer and the Dakotas appeared at Longleat. This was before the famous lions arrived.

Jeanette: They were part of the 'Mersey sound' along with groups like the fantastic Herman's Hermits, Gerry and The Pacemakers and Freddie and The Dreamers. They all wore suits and did a little jig as they played.

Jackie: The 'Mersey Beat' was big. My sister and I 'jammed' with an old wooden guitar and pots and pans for drums to 'Bits and Pieces' by The Dave Clark Five.

Jeanette: We all joined fan clubs. I was a member of the Love Affair fan club.

Jackie: I belonged to The Partridge Family fan club because I loved David Cassidy.

Jeanette: I also had my photo taken with Peter Skellern, who was another local pop star.

Jackie: 'You're a Lady, I'm a Man' was his biggest hit. I have a feeling he worked at the Grosvenor Shaftesbury at one point.

Jeanette: My earliest memory of a music show on TV was Discs A Go-Go. The presenter was Kent Walton who went on to commentate on the wrestling Saturday afternoons. There was also a quite

Jeanette's ticket for a Shaftesbury rock concert featuring local bands in 1971.

amateurish show which was called Thank Your Lucky Stars with Brian Matthew. Then there was Ready Steady Go with Cathy McGowan and also Juke Box Jury with David Jacobs.

Jackie: What was the famous phrase from Thank Your Lucky Stars?

Jeanette: When a girl from Birmingham called Janice Nicholls gave her score, she often said, 'Oi'll give it foive'.

Jackie: When I went to a recording of Top of The Pops at the BBC many years later, I was quite disappointed with the grubby set and the fact that the audience was herded around like cattle.

Jeanette: That's a shame. But in the early days of TOTP there was a girl presenter called Samantha Juste who sat alongside the DJ and pretended to put a record on a turntable each time an act was announced. She married Micky Dolenz from The Monkees.

Jackie: What about Pan's People's dance routines? They always took the lyrics of the song they were dancing to completely literally.

201

'I'd Like To Buy The World A Coke' was a big hit.

Jeanette: I spent a lot of time listening to Radio Luxembourg on a small tinny transistor in my bedroom. The wavelength was 208. It only came on air in the evening.

Jackie: And then Radio One came along. The first record played by DJ Tony Blackburn in 1967 was 'Flowers in the Rain' by The Move. And Sunday nights were when Pick of the Pops with Alan Freeman meant spending a couple of hours with a finger hovering over a cassette recorder to record your favourite songs.

Jeanette: There was genuine suspense during the chart countdown, who'd be top of the charts and make the number one spot?

Jackie: The Monkees, perhaps the first manufactured made-for-TV boy band, was another favourite for me and my sister. Being able to listen to the LP and then watch them on their own TV show made the group very popular. You needed to save hard for an LP and you really felt that you had bought something substantial because as well as the record itself you often got a poster and all the lyrics.

Jeanette: My first LP was 'Tapestry' by Carole King which I played on my brother's little Dansette record player. But I liked Gilbert O'Sullivan too.

Jackie: The first record I bought to play on my red Dansette record player was Puppy Love by Donny Osmond. Singles could be stacked

202

up to five at a time on your record player although sometimes two dropped at once.

Jeanette: Most girls had a special heart-throb though didn't they?

Fab 208 – the official music magazine of Radio Luxembourg featured all the current heartthrobs.

Jackie: Teenage girls like me often picked either David Cassidy or Donny Osmond as their favourite crush. Later on, it was the Bay City Rollers who took the lead in the heart-throb stakes, but I was also fascinated by the strangeness of David Bowie and Marc Bolan of T Rex.

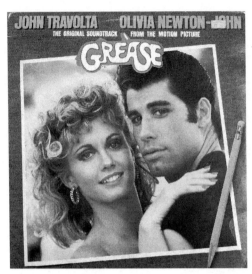

The Grease soundtrack album purchased from Hardings of Shaftesbury for £7.75.

Jeanette: I think there was a little record shop at the bottom of Shaftesbury High Street where you could stand and listen to music in a soundproof booth.

Jackie: Yes, I think there was. Although I also used to visit a record shop in Gillingham with my dad.

Jeanette: It was great to actually see acts in the flesh though wasn't it?

Jackie: Yes, I saw Rod Stewart several times, rocked all over the world with Status Quo and strutted some Tiger Feet with Mud at various venues through the 70s before disco and punk took the pop world in a different direction.

Jeanette: We had holidays in Blackpool where we were lucky enough to see singers like Dusty Springfield and Cilla Black at the Winter Gardens.

Jackie: Lovely to see those big stars.

Jeanette: But I also saw Adge Cutler and the Wurzels and Status Quo at Wincanton Racecourse and on a trip with Shaftesbury Youth Club, we saw Deep Purple at Bournemouth Winter Gardens and also Mott the Hoople who were supported by a then little-known band called Queen.

Jackie: Just goes to show the old ones are the best.

24
What's on The Box?

'I think people thought that TV wouldn't take off!'

Imagine TV when…
Children's programmes are limited to a couple of hours a day.
The National Anthem is played when transmission ends.
There are just two television channels.
There's no colour television.

Jeanette: There were only two TV channels on the first TVs, which were just small wooden boxes.

Jackie: The first TV set we owned had a very small screen housed in a wooden box. It often needed to be given a thump or the vertical or horizontal hold button needed to be fiddled with. TV sets often gave up the ghost and there was much talk of replacing valves and the tube blowing up.

Jeanette: I think people thought that TV wouldn't take off!

Jackie: These were the days before the remote control when you had to get off the sofa to change channels.

Andy Pandy on 'Watch with Mother'.

Jeanette: What do you consider is your earliest memory of watching a programme on TV? Mine's 'Watch with Mother' and puppet characters like Andy Pandy, Bill and Ben and The Woodentops.

Jackie: Me too and it didn't seem to matter that it was all black and white and all the puppets had highly visible strings.

Jeanette: What strings? I thought everything was real.

A postcard from children's TV programme 'Playtime'.

Jeanette: Children's TV was limited to a couple of hours a day with classics such as 'Blue Peter' with presenters like Christopher Trace. I always wanted a Blue Peter badge.

Jackie: And who can forget the Blue Peter Advent Crown? A wire coat hanger wrapped in tinsel and lit with highly dangerous candles!

Sticky back plastic, Fairy Liquid bottles, loo roll tubes which we saved so we could create the latest Blue Peter project.

The bottom of Shaftesbury High Street with Granada Rental on the left where you could watch TV through the shop window. Or pop in and rent one.

Jeanette: Ably demonstrated by Valerie Singleton with 'one I made earlier'.

Jackie: 'It's Friday, it's five past five, it's Crackerjack!' another iconic children's show. Eamonn Andrews hosted in the early days and then it was Leslie Crowther and Peter Glaze.

Jeanette: There was a strange competition where if you gave a wrong answer you had to hold a cabbage. The prize for winners was a Crackerjack pencil.

Jackie: It took place in a theatre.

Jeanette: And they always did a little play at the end.

Jackie: My most favourite shows were those that really captured my imagination like 'Lost in Space', 'Voyage to the Bottom of the Sea', wonderful 'The Man from Uncle', 'The Champions' and puppet shows like 'Joe 90' and 'Thunderbirds'.

Jeanette: I always enjoyed 'Animal Magic' with Johnny Morris voicing all the zoo animals. I much preferred it to 'Zoo Time' with Desmond Morris, which was far more serious.

Jackie: 'Flipper', 'Skippy the Bush Kangaroo', 'Black Beauty', 'Follyfoot' and even 'Tales from the Riverbank' with Hammy the hamster in charge of a tiny speedboat, I watched them all. And in the 70s I watched 'The Partridge Family', which launched the career of heartthrob David Cassidy.

Jeanette: Of course, the first Saturday morning children's TV programme was 'Multi-Coloured Swap Shop' with Noel Edmonds. It was must-see viewing with legendary pop stars in their very early days making appearances.

Jackie: Yes, I always wanted to win one of the big bundles of prizes that were on offer whenever a celebrity guest appeared.

Jeanette: What about programmes we watched as a family? 'Crossroads' was really popular. It was one of the earliest 'soaps' with that unforgettable theme tune composed by Tony Hatch. My cousin, who lived in the Midlands, always said she knew where the Crossroads Motel was. Noel Gordon played motel owner Meg Richardson.

Jackie: There were just three 'wobbly' sets, the kitchen where you might find Amy Turtle, the reception where bobble-hatted Benny might be looking for 'Miss Diane' and Meg's living room where her wheelchair-bound son Sandy was usually having some sort of crisis. The rival motel was called Fairlawns although evidence of its existence was never shown.

Jeanette: Victoria Wood did a great 'take off' of Crossroads with her Acorn Antiques sketches later on.

DJs Tony Blackburn and Noel Edmonds host 'must-watch' Christmas 'Top of the Pops' 1973.

Roy Wood and Wizzard appeared on Christmas 'Top of the Pops' 1973.

'The Morecombe and Wise Show' was classic Christmas TV.

Jackie: I know Mum liked to watch 'Upstairs Downstairs', probably because she'd been in domestic service as a young teenager and because actor John Quayle, a cast member, lived in Compton.

Jeanette: Then there was that ground-breaking documentary called 'Royal Family'. It was amazing to see royalty doing normal things.

Jackie: Yes, we'd never thought of them as 'normal' before. Like Prince Phillip cooking on a barbecue.

Jeanette: There was also Prince Charles' investiture as Prince of Wales. That was at Caernarvon Castle in 1969 and we were given time off school lessons to watch it.

Jackie: The Queen wore an odd hat; it was shaped like a helmet.

Jeanette: Yes, it was strange. But it was good to see the royal family on TV. There was also Princess Anne's wedding to Captain Mark Phillips in 1973.

Jackie: She looked lovely in that high-collared, structured wedding dress.

Jeanette: And there was the Queen's Silver Jubilee in 1977. I loved her bright pink outfit. Lots of street parties were held but I think, as a teenager at the time, I wasn't that interested in what was going on.

Jackie: I watched a lot of American TV programmes such as 'Bonanza' with Hoss and Little Joe. 'The Big Valley', 'The Virginian' and 'The High Chaparral' were also favourites.

Jeanette: And 'Alias Smith and Jones' was brilliant, although the format was copied from 'Butch Cassidy and The Sundance Kid'.

Jackie: British sitcoms like 'On the Buses', 'The Liver Birds', 'Till Death Us Do Part', 'Fawlty Towers', 'Man about the House' and 'Bless this House' were all popular shows which wouldn't see the light of day in this century. All very politically incorrect.

Jeanette: Yes. Whenever I catch old sitcoms on the TV, I'm shocked by the sexism in many of them.

Jackie: They're so bad they're funny. Comedians were also, by today's standards, shockingly sexist. All those mother-in-law jokes, 'er indoors and dumb blonde comments. If any man uttered those words these days, he'd be labelled a 'dinosaur'.

Jeanette: But we thought nothing of watching the Miss World beauty contest.

Jackie: We were always excited to see the contestants who all had to wear white swimsuits and stilettos. Can you believe that during the judging they had to do a 360 degree turn and have their vital statistics broadcast across the world?

Jeanette: Dreadful when you think about it.

Jackie: I think my first memory of watching a big national event on TV was the funeral of Winston Churchill in 1965.

Jeanette: And I think we watched the World Cup in 1966 of course.

'The Man from Uncle' was a 60s and 70s favourite.

Jackie: I know we were still watching on a black and white TV when the moon landings were televised in 1969.

Jeanette: Yes and I liked to watch 'Come Dancing' on Friday nights when I stayed with Nan and Grandad in Shaftesbury. I loved the formation dances. But I think that was in black and white too.

Jackie: The early version of 'Strictly Come Dancing'.

Jeanette: Grandad also liked 'Out of Town' with Jack Hargreaves. And he loved 'The World at War'.

Jackie: That was probably the first documentary series which made an impact. I think it was ground-breaking at the time, the opening titles and stirring music made it memorable.

'Crackerjack' contestants had to balance cabbages when they gave a wrong quiz answer.

Jackie: Nowadays we have hundreds of channels to choose from and watching TV has become far less of a shared experience.

Jeanette: And I still say there's 'nothing to watch!'

25

Hovis…Other Breads Are Available

'The Hovis baker boy pushing his bike up Gold Hill has put the town on the world map..'

Imagine a time when…
Adverts are placed in the local newspaper or on the parish notice board.
You long to make a rocket out of the empty washing-up liquid bottle.
People can't tell the difference between margarine and butter.
Chimpanzees advertise tea.

Jeanette: I often wonder how we advertised things in the days before social media made it as easy as a swipe on our phone.

Jackie: I suppose we must have put a classified advert in the *Western Gazette*, stuck a postcard on the village notice board or went along to one of John Jeffery's auction sales. We had the *Western Gazette* delivered by the 'paper man' every week. It had pages and pages of classified adverts with items for sale, events and cinema listings as well as news stories and full pages of birth, marriage, and death reports.

Jeanette: Jeans sweet shop in Shaftesbury still has a noticeboard outside with postcards advertising things like furniture for sale.

Jackie: Of course, Shaftesbury is the setting for what is probably one of the most iconic adverts of all time. That Hovis baker boy, pushing his bike up Gold Hill has put the town on the world map. As a child I didn't understand why the baker and his boy spoke with a northern accent when they were so obviously in Dorset.

Jeanette: I can't remember them filming that advert. I suppose, because I was a teenager and had other things on my mind, it passed me by.

The notice board remains well used at Jeans Sweet Shop situated in Bell Street, Shaftesbury.

The Hovis TV advert that put Shaftesbury on the world map.

Jackie: Popular TV adverts were frequently more memorable than the programmes in between. I can still sing the Fairy Liquid jingle…'hands that do dishes…'

Jeanette: We always wanted Mum to finish the Fairy Liquid bottle so we could use it for the latest Blue Peter project though, didn't we?

Jackie: Oh yes, to make a rocket!

Jeanette: Soap adverts were certainly very memorable; Ursula Andress advertising Lux soap 'they call her the most beautiful woman in the world' and Katie Boyle demonstrating how creamy Camay was compared to an inferior brand? Mum always said, 'she's very pretty'. I believe she was a countess in real life.

Jackie: And then there was the Colgate toothpaste advert with the 'ring of confidence'. It was a real treat if Mum bought a toothpaste like SR or Signal, with a stripe through it. Shampoos all seemed to start with 'S' – Sunsilk, Supersoft and Silvikrin.

215

Jeanette: In the 70s the 'splash it all over' Brut advert with Henry Cooper was unforgettable and every teenage boy drenched himself in it.

Jackie: We must have used deodorants in the 60s, but I think they were mainly roll-ons.

Jeanette: Mrs Young, the teacher of the middle class at Fontmell Primary School, rubbed a roll-on deodorant stick on our forehead if we had a headache. I suppose it was meant to cool us down and it smelt lovely.

Jackie: The advert for Stork challenged people to tell the difference between margarine and butter. And Homepride flour used little bowler-hatted men as an advertising ploy with the catch line 'graded grains make finer flour'.

Jeanette: Beanz Meanz Heinz is probably one of the most iconic slogans ever and I must admit that Heinz products, whether it's ketchup, soup or salad cream, are still my favourite.

Nan Sims in Shaftesbury bought Nimble bread which I thought was fantastic. The TV advert featured a girl flying off in a balloon to the tune of 'I Can't Let Maggie Go' by a group called Honeybus.

Jackie: Implying that you'd be light enough to float off in a balloon if you ate Nimble.

Jeanette: Some adverts wouldn't pass muster today. For instance, the PG Tips' chimpanzees wouldn't be allowed to move a piano up a staircase these days.

Jackie: True. Animals are much better protected these days.

Jeanette: 'Go to work on an egg' was another unforgettable slogan, and every egg had a little lion stamped on it.

Jackie: Rice Krispies' Snap, Crackle and Pop and the Bisto Kids were unforgettable too. The p..p..pick up a penguin advert is another iconic one.

Jeanette: I always wanted Mum to buy Penguin bars, but we only ever had Taxi wafer bars which were a cheaper version.

Jackie: The 'Maxwell House' coffee ad was very memorable for featuring Michael Caine's wife Shakira. I think he saw the advert, fell in love and has been married to her ever since.

Jeanette: That's so romantic. What about adverts for sweets and chocolate?

Jackie: Bounty gave you 'a taste of paradise?' I'm not sure whether Cadbury can still boast 'a glass and a half of full cream milk in every bar' and who can forget the white-gloved person demonstrating that Treats melted in your mouth, not your hand?

Jeanette: Fry's Turkish Delight was 'full of Eastern promise' and the Cadbury's Flake ad was slightly suggestive. 'A Mars a day helps you work, rest and play', was a slogan apparently created by motor sport presenter, the late Murray Walker.

Jackie: Poor old Joan Collins in the Cinzano advert getting drink spilled on her by Leonard Rossiter, that was a classic. And Schweppes… SSh you know who!

Jackie: The Hamlet advert always reminds me of Dad who always bought a tin of cigars alongside all the Christmas drinks at Eldridge Pope, the off-licence in Shaftesbury High Street. The smell of cigar smoke conjures up Christmas.

Jeanette: Christmas was also a time when you heard 'I'd love a Babycham' and I adored all the 'Bambi' merchandise associated with it.

Jackie: Everyone's glass cabinet seemed to contain some sort of plastic Babycham Bambi.

Jeanette: Aunty Joan ran The Crown at Fontmell and in later years she gave me lots of Babycham glasses.

Jackie: And then there was Pony, 'the little drink with the big kick'.

Jeanette: And Coca Cola 'I'd Like To Buy The World A Coke'.

Jackie: I always wanted to be the glamorous girl in the Martini advert… 'anytime, anyplace, anywhere, that's Martini'. But generally, the woman was put firmly in the kitchen, behind a vacuum cleaner or hanging out the washing.

Jeanette: Well, whatever we think about them, it seems that all these advertising slogans worked on us.

Jackie: And I still read the postcards on the notice board!

26

It's The Most Wonderful Time Of The Year

'The smell of the church candles and the sparkle of tinsel on the angels'
headdresses were part of that heady de-mob happy feeling at the end of term.'

Imagine Christmastime when...
The Morecombe and Wise Show is the highlight of the festive season.
Drawing pins are used to keep decorations in place.
The same Advent calendar is used every year.
Wrapping paper is ironed and recycled.

Jeanette: There's such a big build up to Christmas these days. It seems to start in September.

Jackie: I know, although when we were growing up, we did push the boat out when it came to food, drink and presents at Christmas. What springs to mind about the festive season in Shaftesbury?

Jeanette: The nativity tableaux was outside Shaftesbury Town Hall in a wicker stable with the biblical figures on a bed of straw. The reindeer on top of King Alfred's Kitchen was memorable too.

Jackie: Shaftesbury High Street shops were looking festive although I don't recall 'mulled wine and mince pies' featuring in such a big way as they do today.

Jeanette: I loved the traditional nativity we put on at primary school in St Andrew's Church at Fontmell. Walking down the aisle holding a candle singing 'O Little Town of Bethlehem'. I played Mary in my final year at school. I think there's a newspaper cutting of the event from the *Western Gazette*.

Jackie: I didn't reach the dizzy heights of the virgin Mary although, in my final year, I was given the part of Angel Gabriel. The smell of

FONTMELL MAGNA PLAY

The cast of the Nativity play presented in Fontmell Magna Church by the children of the Primary School. Those who took part included Jeanette Hardim, Kay Merefield, Leslie Pitman, Anthony Trevis, James Strawbridge, Sylvia Weid, Mary Martin, Nicholas Cuff, Shirley and Sue Pitman, Jill Shorten, Elizabeth Lukois, Alan Cuff, Basil Lane, David Jones, Malcolm Lever, Julie Sims, Vanessa Johon and Rowland Hipworth.

Jeanette had the starring role as Mary in Fontmell School's nativity.

the church candles and the wonderful sparkle of tinsel on the angels' headdresses were part of that heady de-mob happy feeling at the end of term.

Jeanette: The school Christmas party was another magical time. The classrooms were candlelit by our own handmade festive candle holders fashioned from bits of wood, plaster of paris, snippets of holly and tinsel and red twisted candles.

Jackie: We each brought in a plate of food, mine was usually chocolate covered marshmallow teacakes, and I wore my sparkly turquoise party dress and black patent shoes. Mum and Dad picked us up on that final day before the Christmas holidays and we went home clutching our handcrafted festive decs and a piece of artwork with one of the tiny calendars attached to the bottom, ready to be gifted to some lucky relative.

Jeanette: Santa's Grotto could usually only be found in the big department stores such as Bobbys in Bournemouth. Woolworths was usually the place to buy your Christmas gifts including the annual tin of Quality Street or Roses. I'm sure they were bigger tins then or maybe it was because I was smaller.

Jackie: The same coronet-style fairy lights were brought out every Christmas and there was the usual testing of the bulbs if they didn't light up. They were multi-coloured, no tasteful soft white LEDs.

Jeanette: Decorations were often simple handmade paper chains or concertina type bells or balls which were pinned to the ceiling. Shinier decs certainly became more common in the 70s and tinsel became available in a range of colours and styles although we kept the same, often threadbare, strands for many years. And all the decorations were attached with drawing pins as this was long before the advent of Blu-Tack®.

Jackie: The tree decorations included real glass baubles and the fairy doll from my childhood still graces my Christmas tree. Mind you, she's now knocking 60 and her lacy white dress which Mum made from an old pair of tights with tinsel trim, is looking a little shabby six decades on. Her aluminium foil-covered wings have been replaced by some snazzy shop-bought fairy wings.

Jeanette: It's so lovely to still have treasured decorations.

Jackie: Our family fairy sat on top of a real Christmas fir tree, which always smelt wonderful. And I still have my very retro plastic Santa Claus who lights up every Christmas. You can tell how old he is by his light brown electric cable that has sticking plaster joins!

Jackie's 60s light up Santa remains a family heirloom.

Jeanette: Our Advent calendars didn't have chocolates or toys in them and the Advent calendar on the classroom wall at Fontmell School was the same every year.

Jackie: At home we also kept the same home-made calendar that Mum made from old Christmas cards cut up and stuck behind a piece of cardboard. But it was still exciting to open each little door every day even though we'd seen each robin, angel or snowman every previous December.

Jeanette: Can you believe my Nan Sims ironed her used wrapping paper and saved it for next Christmas?

Jackie: Habits left over from the war most probably. Wrapping paper was much flimsier then and I loved to receive parcels wrapped with special Christmas tape covered with little robins or sprigs of holly.

Jeanette: On Christmas Eve I think our presents were stuffed in a pillowcase and left at the end of our beds.

Jackie: I don't think I ever believed in Santa, probably because I woke up one Christmas Eve to hear Mum and Dad struggling to get a doll's pram out of the attic.

Jeanette: Which memorable presents did you have growing up? I had a blue and white doll's pram, a desk and chair and several Triang toys when I was very small. Later on, I loved my black jewellery box with a ballerina which played 'Swan Lake'.

Jackie: I always loved to receive an annual.

Jeanette: Aunty Gladys, who worked in WHSmith in Shaftesbury, always gave me an annual, probably *June and Schoolfriend*, *Bunty* or *Judy*.

Jackie: Toiletry sets were popular gifts; bath cubes and talc usually and maybe a 'soap on a rope'.

Jeanette: I loved getting toiletry sets although they often included some disgusting cheap 'scent.'

Jackie: We always had one big gift and lots of little ones, but they were all opened by 10am on Christmas morning while we devoured chocolate from a selection box.

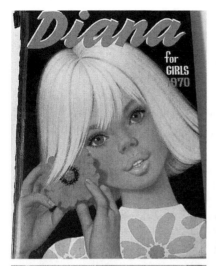

Some of Jackie's annuals.

Jeanette: A chocolate selection box was considered an acceptable present from an aunt or uncle rather than just a stocking filler as it is today.

Jackie: Christmas dinner was eaten at lunchtime, always turkey and all the trimmings with home-made Christmas pud to follow, crackers were pulled, and paper hats worn.

Jeanette: My mum started cooking the dinner on Christmas Eve.

Jackie: After lunch, Dad enjoyed a cigar before falling asleep in his chair before the next round of eating began which would involve things like ham on the bone, turkey sandwiches, home-made trifle and Christmas cake topped with a little plastic Santa, snowman and reindeer, all very faded now, but who still appear on top of my own cake each year.

Jeanette: Nan Sims always made sure she had a tin of 'Ye Olde Oak Ham' (considered a luxury) in the cupboard at Christmas in case of emergencies.

Jackie: And in between courses there was always a bowl of nuts for cracking, and 'Eat Me' dates which Mum loved and ate with the little plastic fork that came in the oval box.

Jeanette: Nobody went out to eat on Christmas Day because pubs, certainly in the 60s, were for drinkers, not diners.

Jackie: It was unheard of to go out to eat. Dad bought a Christmas box of booze from Eldridge Pope, the off-licence in Shaftesbury which probably included bottles of sherry, whisky and brandy, maybe some Dubonnet, Warninks Advocat, Babycham, a barrel of beer or cans of Party Seven and, what I thought was the height of sophistication, a soda syphon. As children we might be treated to a couple of Panda Pops.

Jeanette: Usually, Christmas TV kicked off in the morning with programmes featuring celebrity visits to children's hospital wards which seems quite bizarre looking back. Max Bygraves presented it early on and then it was Michael Aspel and I was always fascinated by the gifts the children were given and wanted to see what they got.

Jackie: Christmas wasn't such a big thing for TV in our childhood.

Jeanette: The 60s and 70s were the golden years for variety and light entertainment though. Shows like 'The Black and White Minstrels' and 'The Billy Cotton Band Show' with that iconic catchphrase 'Wakey Wakey' and also 'Christmas Night with the Stars' with Cilla Black. Cliff Richard, Dusty Springfield, Moira Anderson, Kenneth McKellar. Dick Emery, Mike Yarwood, Ken Dodd were all big names in the 70s.

Jackie: And there were all those popular American shows with Andy Williams and Perry Como.

Jeanette: Although I suppose we had Val Doonican and his rocking chair. He probably started the Christmas jumper craze.

Jackie: And The Young Generation were bouncy young dancers choreographed by Dougie Squires, who seemed to appear on every variety show.

Jeanette: Nan and Grandad Sims always loved 'Holiday on Ice', which was a touring ice-skating show.

Jackie: There was a big film in the afternoon and the Queen's speech. There would be a festive edition of 'The Generation Game' plus 'Top of the Pops' Christmas special, usually shown in the early afternoon, was another one not to be missed.

Jeanette: I couldn't wait to watch the Christmas 'Top of the Pops' with all the number one records from the past year.

Jackie: I think when we were growing up it must have been the golden age for festive songs. What are your earliest memories of Christmas music?

Jeanette: Probably walking down the aisle in Fontmell Church singing 'O Little Town of Bethlehem' in the school nativity.

Jackie: Or 'We Three Kings' or 'Away in a Manger' following someone holding a star on a stick.

Jeanette: That star came out every year.

Jackie: Whenever I hear the descant to 'O Come All Ye Faithful' I think of our Christmas carol services at Shaftesbury High School which were held in Holy Trinity Church.

Jeanette: It was a combined carol service with the boys from the Grammar School so it always created a little bit of excitement. We sat up in the balcony.

Jackie: Launching into the descant of 'Hark the Herald Angels' in a packed church created such a powerful sound. We were all happy as well because it was the end of term.

Jeanette still has some of her annuals.

Jeanette: I was in the choir at Fontmell Church and went carol singing around the village on Christmas Eve. We sang 'The Holly and the Ivy', 'Silent Night' and 'Good King Wenceslas'.

Jackie: You probably wouldn't be allowed to go knocking on people's doors these days. Listening to Carols from Kings on the radio or TV on Christmas Eve is another precursor to the big day.

Jeanette: I don't think I've ever intentionally listened to it, but it's been in the background usually as Mum was preparing festive food in the kitchen on Christmas Eve.

Jackie: Dad came home from the pub on Christmas Eve and got on the piano. He played wartime songs like 'Sentimental Journey' and 'It's a Long Way to Tipperary'. Or my sister, a much better pianist, played some carols for us to sing along to.

Jeanette: Sounds like you were on a par with the Von Trapps! There were lots of songs which couldn't be classed as pop songs, but

Christmas photo shoot with snow scene backdrop for Jeanette and brother David.

that have been popular for decades, like 'Jingle Bells'; 'Rocking around the Christmas Tree'; 'I Saw Mummy Kissing Santa Claus'; 'Most Wonderful Time of the Year' and 'White Christmas'.

Jackie: And all the Phil Spector productions such as 'Frosty the Snowman', 'Santa Claus Is Coming To Town' have been popular for decades.

Jeanette: It was the 70s that were the golden years for Christmas hits though, like Slade's 'Merry Christmas Everybody'.

Jackie: Noddy Holder must be still living off the royalties. One of my favourites is 'I Believe In Father Christmas' by Greg Lake. Even though the video was apparently shot in the desert, the song reminds me of a white Christmas in Compton.

Jeanette: I think my favourite is Joni Mitchell's 'The River' and 'Ring Out Solstice Bells' by Jethro Tull. I didn't really like 'Mull of Kintyre'. But I was fascinated by the video of Wizzard's 'I Wish it Could Be Christmas Every Day' and Roy Wood's long coloured hair.

Jackie: 'Step into Christmas' by Elton John, 'Happy Christmas War is Over' by John Lennon, Mud's 'Lonely This Christmas', they're all iconic 70s Christmas hits.

Jeanette: Bing Crosby and David Bowie singing 'Peace on Earth' was an odd pairing, wasn't it?

Jackie: Apparently, they didn't get on at all.

Jeanette: But Cliff is a perennial favourite, isn't he? 'Mistletoe and Wine', 'Saviours Day' and all those cheesy videos.

Jackie: How about Boney M's 'Mary's Boy Child'? They wore all those boa-feather trimmed Santa outfits.

Jeanette: I never liked Boney M. But I always loved 'The Twelve Days of Christmas' especially when you reached the 'Five Gold Rings' part!

Jackie: Apart from listening to all that Christmas music, we also played cards and board games as well as charades which was always a winner.

Jeanette: Boxing Day was much more relaxed and was the day to get out for a walk if the weather was good.

Jackie: There was bubble and squeak for breakfast and all the delicious leftovers like cold meats with mashed potato, cheese and pickles, turkey sandwiches (again), mince pies and maybe some chocolate yule log.

Jeanette: Christmas is all about nostalgia. I love to bring out all the old decorations and continue the traditions from my childhood. It's really comforting.

Jackie: I think it really was a special time when we were growing up because, unlike today, we didn't indulge ourselves in the same way throughout the rest of the year.

And it's goodbye from us...

In 1979, both of us left Shaftesbury to take on new challenges and seek new adventures.

Strangely, at that time, we weren't very close and were completely unaware of each other's plans. We left the town, heading for different destinations, never realising that years later we'd both return, get to know each other better and realise how much, as cousins, we have in common.

It's been a joy to reconnect, join together and write about our experiences growing up in Dorset.

We truly hope our book evokes lots of nostalgia for you as we've brought to life our wonderful, often amusing and undoubtedly precious, memories of life in the 60s and 70s.

Index

Printed in Poland
by Amazon Fulfillment
Poland Sp. z o.o., Wrocław

34715002R00132